THE SIEGE OF JERUSALEM

THE SIEGE
OF JERUSALEM

a *Broadview Anthology of British Literature* edition

Contributing Editor and Translator, *The Siege of Jerusalem*:
Adrienne Williams Boyarin, University of Victoria

General Editors,
Broadview Anthology of British Literature:
Joseph Black, University of Massachusetts, Amherst
Leonard Conolly, Trent University
Kate Flint, University of Southern California
Isobel Grundy, University of Alberta
Don LePan, Broadview Press
Roy Liuzza, University of Tennessee
Jerome J. McGann, University of Virginia
Anne Lake Prescott, Barnard College
Barry V. Qualls, Rutgers University
Claire Waters, University of California, Davis

broadview press

Library and Archives Canada Cataloguing in Publication
Siege of Jerusalem (Middle English poem). English
    The siege of Jerusalem / contributing editor and translator,
The siege of Jerusalem: Adrienne Williams Boyarin, University of
Victoria ; general editors, Broadview Anthology of British Literature:
Joseph Black, University of Massachusetts, Amherst, Leonard Conolly,
Trent University, Kate Flint, University of Southern California, Isobel
Grundy, University of Alberta, Don LePan, Broadview Press, Roy Liuzza,
University of Tennessee, Jerome J. McGann, University of Virginia, Anne
Lake Prescott, Barnard College, Barry V. Qualls, Rutgers University, Claire
Waters, University of California, Davis. — A Broadview anthology of British
literature edition.

Translated from the Middle English.
Includes bibliographical references.
ISBN 978-1-55481-158-8 (pbk.)

    1. Jerusalem—History—Siege, 70 A.D.—Poetry. I. Boyarin, Adrienne
Williams, writer of added commentary, editor, translator II. Title.

PR2065.S513 2013   821'.1   C2013-907246-2

Broadview Press is an independent, international publishing house, incorporated in 1985.

We welcome comments and suggestions regarding any aspect of our publications—please feel free to contact us at the addresses below or at broadview@broadviewpress.com.

North America	PO Box 1243, Peterborough, Ontario, Canada K9J 7H5 2215 Kenmore Ave., Buffalo, New York, USA 14207 Tel: (705) 743-8990; Fax: (705) 743-8353 email: customerservice@broadviewpress.com
UK, Europe, Central Asia, *Middle East, Africa, India,* *and Southeast Asia*	Eurospan Group, 3 Henrietta St., London WC2E 8LU, UK Tel: 44 (0) 1767 604972; Fax: 44 (0) 1767 601640 email: eurospan@turpin-distribution.com
Australia and New Zealand	NewSouth Books, c/o TL Distribution 15-23 Helles Ave., Moorebank, NSW, Australia 2170 Tel: (02) 8778 9999; Fax: (02) 8778 9944 email: orders@tldistribution.com.au

www.broadviewpress.com

Developmental Editors: Jennifer McCue and Laura Buzzard

Broadview Press acknowledges the financial support of the Government of Canada through the Canada Book Fund for our publishing activities.

PRINTED IN CANADA

For Shamma באהבה

Contents

Acknowledgments

I am grateful to my students at the University of Victoria, who have thought through *The Siege of Jerusalem* with me many times, and particularly to Danica Boyce, Alyssa McLeod, and Daniel Powell, who, in a Fall 2011 graduate seminar on anti-Jewish discourses in medieval England, engaged me in long and intellectually rigorous discussions of this text, its editions, and our varying in-class translations. Their smart questions about the nature of access and canonicity ultimately convinced me that pursuing the present little volume was important. My thanks also to colleagues Iain Higgins and J. Allan Mitchell, who commented usefully on drafts, particularly of introductory materials and headnotes; to my three press readers, who offered generous support and constructive suggestions at breakneck speed; and to Shamma Boyarin especially, who read everything and translated two of the Hebrew "In Context" items. Don LePan, Jennifer McCue, Merilee Atos, and Kaitlyn Till at Broadview Press have my gratitude for their patience and, of course, for all they do at Broadview to support university teachers and facilitate the publication process. I have benefited also from the help of three research assistants: Alyssa McLeod, David Carlton, and Nathan Phillips. By far my greatest debts are to Ralph Hanna, David Lawton, and Michael Livingston, whose editions of *The Siege of Jerusalem* appeared about a decade ago. Their years of research and editorial labor enabled my much more menial work here, and the whole is a gesture of appreciation.

Permission was generously granted for use of the following "In Context" materials:

Selections from the Middle English *Siege of Jerusalem* edited by Ralph Hanna and David Lawton, copyright © 2003 Oxford University Press for the Early English Text Society, are reprinted by permission of the publisher. Selections from William Granger Ryan's two-volume translation of Jacobus Voragine's *Legenda aurea*, *The Golden Legend: Readings on the Saints*, copyright © 1993 Princeton University Press, are reprinted by permission of the publisher. The selection from Shlomo Eidelberg's translation of Eliezar bar Nathan's crusade chronicle, from *The Jews and the Crusaders: The Hebrew Chronicles of the First and*

Preface

> I will not cease from Mental Fight,
> Nor shall my Sword sleep in my hand:
> Till we have built Jerusalem
> In England's green & pleasant Land.
> —William Blake, from the preface to *Milton*

The medieval poem translated here is part of a long tradition of thinking about Jerusalem in England and in English, though it is also an artifact of international and intercultural engagement. Its story of Rome's movement eastward and Jerusalem's movement westward matters to an understanding of what many writers and thinkers in the western tradition are doing with Jerusalem, a city always a mappable location, historically a place of conquest and conflict, and a symbolic place of "mental fight."

The current Middle English editions of the alliterative *Siege of Jerusalem*—published by Ralph Hanna and David Lawton in 2003, and by Michael Livingston in 2004—are broadly suitable to scholarly, graduate, and advanced undergraduate reading. The present volume, however, is the poem's first rendering in Modern English and is meant for a wider audience. Both blatantly literary and an ethical failure, *Siege* had received little critical attention before the 1990s. Hanna is very often quoted for his comment that it "has a perfectly deserved reputation as the chocolate-covered tarantula of the [late-medieval] alliterative movement,"[1] by which we might understand that it is at once sweetly adorned and dangerous, or ugly. And so it is. Yet my hope in translating, introducing, and contextualizing it for a broad readership is that it will be more frequently queried in terms of the intellectual and literary histories of which it is, also, a part.

The translation and annotations here should serve as good companions to the Middle English editions. Throughout, I have striven to remain true to the Middle English text, so that any reader wishing to do more advanced work can reliably move between the volumes and find not contradiction but expansion and productive complication.

---

1 "Contextualising *The Siege of Jerusalem*," *Yearbook of Langland Studies* 6 (1992): 109.

In so striving, I have relied both on my own experiences teaching the text and, necessarily and heavily, on the labor of others. In annotations and in cases of difficult-to-render lines or stanzas, I have frequently adopted the explanations of previous editors, and I have privileged Hanna and Lawton in this regard. The Middle English excerpts included with the "In Context" materials also follow Hanna and Lawton's text. What is presented here, in other words, is digested: it uses available scholarship to make an important poem understandable. *Siege* can be troublesome for new readers on multiple levels, and this volume takes into account interested readers who may have little or no previous knowledge of the medieval period, the first-century events that the poem evokes, or the literary contexts of late-fourteenth-century England.

The works collected in the "In Context" section aim to introduce some of the linguistic, biblical, legendary, literary, and historical circumstances that produced and surrounded *The Siege of Jerusalem*, though the collection is by no means complete and is inevitably inflected by my own areas of research and knowledge. While most of what is here can be found online or anthologized in many other (disparate) places, there are some new translations interspersed, and I hope that it will prove useful for students and teachers to have these materials gathered and augmented by new annotation. In my compiling efforts, I have privileged the less accessible or less frequently taught. I have not, for instance, attempted to provide much of the alliterative context (i.e., what might be taught in a course on alliterative traditions or "revivals"), since it is very well represented elsewhere, and many teaching texts, both in Middle English and in Modern English translation, are available for the central works of that tradition.

In rendering this poem into Modern English verse, I have attempted the hat trick of faithful and readable translation; maintenance of the poem's distinctive vocabulary, ambiguities, and repetitions; and representation of its original alliterative aesthetic. Students will be able to use the translation alongside the Middle English editions, as I have retained their line-to-line and stanza-to-stanza breaks and not strayed far from the literal, though of course there are instances where Modern English syntax or style matters have made this impossible. I have also tried to avoid supplying or unnecessarily correcting ambiguous pronouns, to maintain the poet's word order and word play where possible (e.g., in cases of verbal echo or delayed subjects), and generally to avoid forcing interpretation onto the process of translating. While I am certain that I have not always succeeded, I have been much informed by my own pedagogical wishes for translations: that they be readable in their own right but also allow for textual analysis and formal critical inquiry that will remain relevant should a student progress to more advanced work in the original language.

Ideally we have the ability to read and use texts in multiple ways and in multiple contexts, and, overall, my aim has been simply to create new possibilities for *The Siege of Jerusalem*, and particularly for teachers whose pedagogical goals are not (or not always) language-based or bound by medieval or literary studies.

Adrienne Williams Boyarin
Victoria, BC

Introduction

This is not the heavenly Jerusalem, but the one down below,
way down below. And from the sea floor, they dredge up
    ruined walls
and fragments of faiths, like rust-colored vessels from sunken
prophecy ships. That's not rust, it's blood that has never dried.
And clay jars covered with seaweed, the corals of time and the
    fury of time
and coins from days gone by, the negotiable currency of the
    past.
    —Yehuda Amichai, "Jerusalem, Jerusalem, Why Jerusalem?"

The Siege of Jerusalem (c. 1370–90 CE) is a difficult text. By twenty-first-century standards, it is gruesomely violent and offensive. It tells the story of the Roman destruction of the Second Temple in Jerusalem in 70 CE, an event viewed by its author (as by many in the Middle Ages) as divine retribution against Jews for the killing of Christ. It anachronistically turns first-century Roman emperors Titus and Vespasian into Christian converts who battle like medieval crusaders to avenge their savior and cleanse the Holy Land of enemies of the faith. It makes little sense without frank understanding of medieval Christian anti-Semitism, and its depictions of violent conquest must also be considered in relation to the crusade campaigns in which Western Europe was involved throughout the period.[1] There is, nevertheless, some consensus that *Siege* is a finely crafted piece of poetry, and that its combination of horror, beauty, and learnedness makes it an effective work of art. As literary scholar A.C. Spearing has put it, "We may not like what the poet does, but it is done with skilful craftsmanship and sometimes with brilliant virtuosity."[2]

The tale that the anonymous *Siege* poet tells, moreover, is an important and still reverberating part of the history of western thinking

---

1   Fourteenth-century political and military crises and conflicts between England and France are also relevant. See Michael Livingston's introduction to his edition of *Siege of Jerusalem* (Kalamazoo: Medieval Institute, 2004), especially 24–30, and Suzanne Yeager's *Jerusalem in Medieval Narrative* (Cambridge: Cambridge UP, 2008).

2   "Alliterative Poetry," in *Readings in Medieval Poetry* (Cambridge: Cambridge UP, 1987), 167.

about the East. It is, to use Yehuda Amichai's phrase, a "currency of the past" that continues to be negotiated. The first-century destruction of Jerusalem has been understood in both Christian and Jewish traditions as the beginning of the Jewish Diaspora, and for medieval Christians it was also a model of successful Christian leadership and justified warfare, an allegory of political and personal spiritual battle. As part of the story of the historical rift between Christianity and Judaism, the destroyed Second Temple came to be symbolic of the fall of Judaism and the rise of the new Christian era in which anyone who rejected Christ would suffer. In the Middle Ages, such thinking extended to general consideration of religious and ethnic difference, the cost and justification of crusade expeditions, and the question of what exactly Christians defined themselves against. Stories of the devastation of Jerusalem were crafted as stories of the "Vengeance of Our Lord," and they were internationally popular in poetry, prose, and drama.[1]

The fundamentally anti-Jewish narrative of *The Siege of Jerusalem* is a large part of what makes it uncomfortable reading. When the poet begins with the torture and death of Jesus in Roman-controlled Judea, he begins with an event that was, nearly universally in medieval Western Christendom, blamed on Jews. The combination of this accusation with later medieval devotional movements that emphasized the humanity of Christ meant that Jews could be openly reviled and deemed punishable in the poet's time, uneasily situated as both coreligionists and killers of Jesus. In twelfth- and thirteenth-century England, persecutions of Jews included violent attacks and legal and professional marginalization, and culminated in forced expulsion by King Edward I in 1290. Libelous narratives about medieval Jews included the accusation that they desecrated the consecrated Host and secretly ritually murdered young Christian boys.[2] At the same time, medieval Christians were well aware that Christianity developed out of Judaism, that Jesus and his mother and disciples were Jewish, that

---

1   See for example Steven K. Wright, *The Vengeance of Our Lord: Medieval Dramatizations of the Destruction of Jerusalem* (Toronto: Pontifical Institute, 1989); Alvin E. Ford, ed., *La Vengeance de Nostre-Seigneur: The Old and Middle French Prose Versions*, 2 vols. (Toronto: Pontifical Institute, 1984–93); and J.A. Herbert, ed., *Titus & Vespasian: or, The Destruction of Jerusalem in Rhymed Couplets.* Roxburghe Club 146 (London: Roxburghe Club, 1905).
2   See "In Context" section D, below, for samples of related texts.

Hebrew scriptures were the foundation of Christian scripture and prophecy, and that patriarchs and matriarchs of Christianity were likewise patriarchs and matriarchs of Judaism. Many religious thinkers believed that Jews deserved "relative tolerance" as the recipients of the first covenant of God and as witnesses to Christian salvation.[1] This familial intimacy resulted in ambivalent representation of Jews in literature and art, and in representation of Judaism and Jewish customs that frequently emphasized blame and difference at the cost of truthfulness.

The portrayal of Jews in *Siege* is additionally complicated by the influence of crusader accounts of travel and warfare in the Holy Land. Jerusalem as a place and "Jew" as a category could acquire blurred boundaries and histories in this light. While the religious and military justification of crusades lay in the perceived right of Christians to "reclaim" territory from Muslims, for instance, in practice crusade campaigns also included massacres of European Jews by crusaders traveling to Jerusalem, who, according to one chronicler of the First Crusade, believed such attacks "to be the beginning of their expedition and their duty."[2] While the *Siege* poet draws on chronicles of first-century Roman-Jewish conflicts and considers Judaism in its scriptural and historical relationship with Christianity, he also clearly knew stories of the 1099 CE crusader conquest of Jerusalem, and of later attempts to hold or regain the city, and sometimes seems to describe the political and religious narratives of medieval European and Roman (papal) encounters with the Muslim and Arab East.[3]

There are, in other words, fantastical and provocatively anachronistic combinations of histories, peoples, places, and times in *The*

---

[1] On the tradition of relative tolerance and its theological bases, see Jeremy Cohen, "The Doctrine of Jewish Witness," in *Living Letters of the Law: Ideas of the Jew in Medieval Christianity* (Berkeley: U of California P, 1999), 23–65.

[2] From Albert of Aachen's *History of the Journey to Jerusalem* (written c. 1125–50). See "In Context" section D.1 for excerpts of this and other crusade chronicles.

[3] On medieval conflations of Jew and Muslim, with attention to *The Siege of Jerusalem* and the influence of crusade histories, see Suzanne Akbari, "Placing the Jews in Late Medieval English Literature," in *Orientalism and the Jews*, ed. Ivan Davidson Kalmar and Derek Jonathan Penslar (Lebanon, NH: Brandeis UP, 2005), 30–50. On the popular romance imagination of Jews and Muslims in medieval England, see Geraldine Heng, "The Romance of England: *Richard Coer de Lyon*, Saracens, Jews, and the Politics of Race and Nation," in *The Postcolonial Middle Ages*, ed. Jeffrey Jerome Cohen (New York: St Martin's, 2000): 135–71.

Siege of Jerusalem: Romans, Christians, Jews, Muslims, first-century wars and medieval crusades, England and France (where we first meet Titus), Rome and Judea—and more. Alongside the poem's violence and anti-Jewish rhetoric, this fact is (and maybe always was to some extent) destabilizing for readers. Without some mindfulness of the admixtures and their associated ambivalences, it is hard to understand how the *Siege* poet can so often seem to delight in the torture and death of his Jewish characters and celebrate Roman prowess and faith, yet at other times depict Roman attackers as inhumane and excessive. He may dismiss Jews as "faithless," "false," or "heathen," yet at other moments express sympathy with Jewish suffering and describe Jewish characters as "brave," "fair," or "noble." It is occasionally hard to distinguish Christians or Romans from Jews, and it frequently seems that the author has ignorantly consigned Jews to a monolithic and exoticized "Eastern" identity. The *Siege* poet has, instead, carefully created Christian and Jewish parallels that simultaneously expose similarities and differences, all the while negotiating his paradigm of Christian history and prophecy, long-established stereotypes of Roman excellence and excess, and popularized Arab "oriental" settings of the Holy Land associated by his time with crusading literature and Christian heroics.

The Text and Its Sources

The Siege of Jerusalem was clearly popular in its own time. It survives in whole or in fragments in nine fourteenth- and fifteenth-century copies, and, in terms of its verse and production, it is not an atypical text. Like some of the more frequently taught poems of the same period—*Sir Gawain and the Green Knight* (and its companion texts *Pearl*, *Cleanness*, and *Patience*) and William Langland's *Piers Plowman* among them—the anonymous *Siege* was written in Middle English alliterative verse and composed in the late fourteenth century. But *Sir Gawain* and its companions, by comparison, survive in a single manuscript, and the only alliterative poem of the period to survive in more copies than *Siege* is *Piers Plowman*.

Like most medieval texts, *Siege* was likely never encountered on its own: in the manuscripts that have survived, it is anthologized, and thus, as its editors Ralph Hanna and David Lawton caution, a "one-volume presentation of *The Siege* differs decidedly from any medieval experience of the work."[1] It exists in codices alongside other English alliterative poems and romances (twice it appears with *Piers Plowman*), but also with Latin prose histories, devotional and scriptural pieces, works of moral and spiritual instruction, and secular verse. Aspects of the religious and political backdrop described above might come into greater or lesser relief depending on its codiciological contexts.[2]

The poem's meter is the alliterative long line. In the original Middle English, each line relies on stressed patterns of initial sounds organized around a central caesura, with the standard pattern aa(a)/ax. This, similar to Old English alliterative verse, is an unrhymed oral style, driven by sound, rhythm, and formulaic patterns and phrases, but it does not necessarily follow that *Siege* was composed orally or received only by listening audiences. Rather, "the opposites of bookishness and orality" are part of what characterizes *Siege*, both in form and content.[3] The poet was probably a learned canon at an Augustinian monastery in Yorkshire,[4] writing for secular patrons, and, like other English poets working at this time, he was skilled at interweaving his poetic style with bookish historical, theological, and legendary sources.[5]

Partly because of the strict demands of alliterative verse, *Siege* echoes several English alliterative poems of its age and, particularly, poems concerned with historical events, heroic deeds, and warfare (especially the long poems known as *The Gest Hystoriale of the Destruction of Troy*, *The Wars of Alexander*, and the alliterative *Morte Arthure*). A good comparative example is found, for instance, in a passage from *The Destruction of Troy* that describes the bolting of city gates after battle. In *Siege*, these lines describe the Jews who have been driven within the walls of Jerusalem by the Romans:

---

1   *The Siege of Jerusalem* (Oxford: Oxford UP, 2003), xxvii.
2   For details on the surviving copies of the poem, along with manuscript descriptions and summaries of contents and arrangements, see Hanna and Lawton, xiii–xxvii.
3   Ibid., lxxvi.
4   On the significance of the Yorkshire context to the poem's anti-Judaism and crusading interests, see Andrew Galloway, "Alliterative Poetry in Old Jerusalem: *The Siege of Jerusalem* and its Sources," in *Medieval Alliterative Poetry: Essays in Honour of Thorlac Turville-Petre*, ed. John A. Burrow and Hoyt N. Duggan (Dublin: Four Courts, 2010), 85–106.
5   See "In Context" section A for more on the poem's author, manuscripts, and verse.

Ledes lepen to anon, louken þe ȝates,	At once men rush forward to fasten the gates,
Barren hem bigly with boltes of yren;	Bolt them up firmly with big iron bars,
Brayden vp brigges with brouden chaynes	Tug up the drawbridges with twisted-link chains (617–19)[1]

In *The Destruction of Troy*, these lines describe the Trojans who have been driven inside the walls of Troy by the Greeks:

Þei wan in wightly, warpit þe yates,	They fled inside quickly, threw down the gates,
Barrit hom full bigly with boltes of yerne;	Bolted them up very firmly with big iron bars;
Braid vp the brigges in a breme hast	Tugged up the drawbridges in a great haste (10462–64)[2]

Illustrative instances of shared formulae and vocabulary are apparent in other alliterative poems as well. Comparison of the Roman fleet in *Siege* and King Arthur's fleet in *Morte Arthure* shows nearly identical naval vocabulary used to describe ships of various size and utility: in *Siege* there are "floynes aflot, farcostes many, / Cogges and crayers, ycasteled alle" (floines set afloat, and farcosts many, / Cogs and crayers, with battlements all) (289–90), and in *Morte Arthure* "Coggez and crayers … floynes and fercostez and Flemesche schyppes" (Cogs and crayers … floines and farcosts and Flemish ships) (738, 743).[3] Elsewhere the *Siege* poet describes "arwes … with attyr enuenymyd" (arrows … with poison envenomed) during battle (658), matching the "Archars with arows of attir envemonde" (Archers with arrows envenomed by poison) in *The Wars of Alexander* (1513).[4]

---

1 The Middle English text follows Hanna and Lawton.
2 *The Gest Hystoriale of the Destruction of Troy*, ed. George A. Panton and David Donaldson, 2 vols. (London: Trübner, 1869–74).
3 *Morte Arthure: A Critical Edition*, ed. Mary Hamel (New York and London: Garland, 1984).
4 *The Wars of Alexander*, ed. Hoyt N. Duggan and Thorlac Turville-Petre (Oxford: Oxford UP, 1989).

This very small sampling of apparent textual relations is sufficient to show why scholars working on *Siege* have speculated about the degree of influence of these texts and authors upon one another, even about their relative dates of composition or the possibilities of shared authorship or local affiliations. Such echoes are so suggestive that it was once believed that the *Siege* poet mimicked the others, though it is now generally accepted that the case is the reverse, that *Siege* is the earlier text influencing others.[1] Within a poetic style that is by definition interested in creating and playing with patterns, however, it is not easy to trace lines of dissemination or determine who was reading what. It is as likely that these poets participated in a shared regional tradition as it is that they borrowed directly from one another. We can say, at least, that the *Siege* poet was working within a particular literary milieu that also included the other works mentioned here.

The poem's story is certainly not derived from any other English poem.[2] In the main, it is a synthesis of three narratives (gleaned from multiple sources) that were widely known in the Middle Ages, predominantly in prose: the story of the Roman siege of Jerusalem by Titus and Vespasian; the legend of St. Veronica, a woman who offered her veil that Jesus might wipe his face (the veil cloth, known as the "Vernicle," miraculously held the image of Jesus' face and afterwards performed miracles itself); and the story of the death of Christ, as told in the gospels and in apocryphal legend. The *Siege* poet was not the first to put these together. While it is clear that he knew well and relied on biblical narrative,[3] he found the full outline of his story elsewhere. His sources, direct or indirect, included the *Legenda aurea*, or *Golden Legend*, a thirteenth-century Latin collection of readings

---

1   Hanna and Lawton make this case and review the scholarly history in *The Siege*, xxxv-xxxviii. See also Livingston, 10–15, who sees particularly strong links between *Siege* and *The Destruction of Troy* and *Morte Arthure*, and allows for shared authorship with the latter on 28–30.

2   The Middle English poem known as *Titus and Vespasian* was composed roughly contemporaneously with *Siege*, but it is significantly longer, draws on different narrative traditions, and is written in rhyming couplets. Apart from shared subject matter, there is very little evidence of textual relationship. See Maija Birenbaum, "Affective Vengeance in *Titus and Vespasian*," *Chaucer Review* 43.3 (2009): 330–44.

3   For some of the most important biblical passages underpinning the poem, see "In Context" section B.

about the saints;[1] the *Vindicata salvatoris*, or *Vengeance of the Savior*, a popular Latin legendary account of Titus, Vespasian, and St. Veronica that circulated from the eighth century and was itself the product of compiled legends about its main characters; and Roger d'Argenteuil's *Bible en françois*, a thirteenth-century French prose selection of Bible stories and related moralizing commentary and tales, including the story of the healing of Vespasian and his vengeful war against Jerusalem.[2] The poet also used up to three historical accounts of the Roman-Jewish War: first-century Jewish historian Flavius Josephus' *Wars of the Jews* (which the poet would have known in a Latin redaction); English monk Ranulf Higden's fourteenth-century *Polychronicon*, a long Latin history of the world according to Christian scriptural and theological perspectives, which itself made use of the redacted works of Josephus; and Yorkshire chronicler John of Tynemouth's fourteenth-century *Historia aurea*, or *Golden History*, a very long Latin history of the Christian world and Britain through the 1340s, heavily indebted to Higden's *Polychronicon*.[3]

The poet is sometimes more or less directly translating from his sources, as we can see by his use of the first sentence of *Vindicta salvatoris* in the opening lines of *Siege*:

In the days of emperor Tiberius Caesar, while Herod was tetrarch, under Pontius Pilate the Lord was delivered by the Jews, unbeknownst to Tiberius.[4]

In the time of Tiberius, Sir Caesar true,
The rightful emperor who ruled in Rome,
When Pilate was provost under that rich prince
And also judge of Jews in Judean lands,

---

1   For more information on *The Golden Legend*, including relevant excerpts, see "In Context" section C.

2   This tale is also known separately as the *Vengeance de nostre Seigneur*. The *Bible en françois* version is introduced and edited in Ford, *La Vengeance*, vol. 2, 74–138.

3   On the poet's dependence on John of Tynemouth, see Galloway, "Alliterative Poetry in Old Jerusalem," who shows that details from Josephus, Higden, and *The Golden Legend* were already combined in the *Historia aurea*'s account of the siege.

4   Translated from Hanna and Lawton's edition of the Latin text in *The Siege*, "Appendix A: The Vindicta Salvatoris," 160. See also Bart D. Ehrman and Zlatko Plese, ed. and trans., *The Apocryphal Gospels: Texts and Translations* (Oxford and New York: Oxford UP, 2011), 537–58.

Herod, under his rule, and by hereditary right,
Was called king of Galilee, when Christ died.
Though Caesar was spotless (he hated sin),
Through Pilate He was pained and put on the rood. (1–8)

It remains undoubtedly true, however, that the process of versifying
and translating is a creative one, as is the process of combining and ar-
ranging various sources of differing genres and viewpoints. The *Siege*
poet, as he translates and conflates his sources into a rhythmic and
emotive English alliterative poetry, creates an integrated (and there-
fore new) story of the 70 CE fall of Jerusalem.

One particularly disturbing scene of starvation inside the besieged
Jerusalem may serve to make this final point. Late in the poem, the
Siege poet describes a Jewish mother named Mary who is so hungry
and despairing that she cooks and eats her own son (1081–1100).
This episode is hardly new. It was first recorded by Josephus in his
purportedly eyewitness account of the siege, and it was, by the poet's
time, a set-piece in visual and literary renderings of the destruction of
Jerusalem and the Second Temple.[1] This episode of maternal canni-
balism appears in four of the poet's possible sources: in Josephus' *Wars
of the Jews*, but also in *The Golden Legend*, Higden's *Polychronicon*,
and John of Tynemouth's *Historia aurea*, all of which, in turn, used
Josephus directly or indirectly. Here is the episode as it appears in
Josephus:

There was a certain woman that dwelt beyond Jordan, her name
was Mary…. and it was now become impossible for her any
way to find any more food, while the famine pierced through
her very bowels and marrow. When also her passion was fired
to a degree beyond the famine itself, and she consulted with
nothing but with her passion and the necessity she was in, she
then attempted a most unnatural thing; and snatching up her
son, which was sucking at her breast, she said, "O thou mis-
erable infant! for whom shall I preserve thee in this war, this

---

1   See Merrall Llewelyn Price, "Imperial Violence and the Monstrous Mother: Cannibalism at
the Siege of Jerusalem," in *Domestic Violence in Medieval Texts*, ed. Eve Salisbury, Georgiana
Donavin, and Merrall Llewelyn Price (Gainesville: UP of Florida, 2002), 272–98.

famine, and this sedition? As to the war with the Romans, if they preserve our lives, we must be slaves. This famine also will destroy us, even before that slavery comes upon us. Yet are these seditious rogues more terrible than both the other. Therefore, be thou my food; and be thou a fury to these seditious varlets, and a by-word to the world, which is all that is now wanting to complete the calamities of us Jews." As soon as she had said this, she slew her son, and then roasted him, and ate the one half of him, and kept the other half concealed. Upon this the seditious came in presently; and smelling the scent of this food, they threatened her that they would cut her throat immediately, if she did not show them what food she had gotten ready. She replied that she had saved a very fine portion of it for them: and at the same time uncovered what was left of her son. Hereupon they were seized with a horror, and amazement; and stood astonished at the sight: when she said to them, "This is mine own son: and what hath been done was mine own doing. Come, eat of this food; for I have eaten of it myself. Do not you pretend to be either more tender than a woman, or more compassionate than a mother. But if you be so scrupulous, and abominate this my sacrifice, as I have eaten the one half, let the rest be reserved for me also." At these words the men went out trembling, being never so much affrighted at any thing as they were at this, and with some difficulty they left the rest of that meat to the mother.[1]

Some details of this account seem to make it into the *Siege* poet's version of the episode—the mob's threat that they will kill Mary for concealing food, the chilling effect of the scene on those who approach—but some details clearly derive from reliance either on Higden's *Polychronicon* or John of Tynemouth's *Historia*, particularly Mary's instruction to her son, which reads in both Englishmen's chronicles, "Redi in id secretum a quo existi" ("Return to that se-

---

1   William Whiston, trans., *The Complete Works of Flavius Josephus* (London: Nelson, 1860), from *War of the Jews* VI.3.4, with some minor adjustments to punctuation. A very readable more recent translation is available in Gaalya Cornfeld, ed. and trans., *Josephus: The Jewish War* (Grand Rapids, MI: Zondervan, 1982).

cret place from which you came"). [1] What is more, the poet certainly knew the version of the episode told in the internationally popular *Golden Legend*, which shares details with Josephus, Higden, and John of Tynemouth, but relies only indirectly on Josephus and predates the two fourteenth-century chronicles. [2]

Deciding with certainty the degree of knowledge, borrowing, and translation of each possible source—or rejecting the thought that the poet might have experienced other versions of the story as well, for instance in illustrations or dramas that no longer survive—is almost impossible. Yet the poet clearly creates something new when he renders the episode in his English vernacular, in alliterative long lines, and with his own few unique details:

> One Mary, a mild woman, because of absence of food,
> Cooked on the coals her own baby, whom she bore.
> She roasts the spine and the ribs, with pitiful words,
> Says: "Son, upon each side is our sorrow increased:
>
> Battle is outside the city to slaughter our bodies,
> Hunger is so hot within that our hearts nearly burst.
> Therefore give up what I gave you, and turn back again,
> Enter where you came out"—and she eats a shoulder. (1081–88) [3]

The cinematic focus on the spine and ribs on coals, the momentary misdirection when "upon each side" seems to refer to roasting meat rather than the sorrow of the siege, the doubled attack on the body politic and corporeal body that Mary laments, the internal and external violence that simultaneously describes city and body in a concentric relationship—all of these are the result of the poet's craft. His shift from past tense description into the historical present tense that

---

1 See Hanna and Lawton's "Appendix B: Higden's Polychronicon," in *The Siege*, 164–69, here 168; and Galloway's edition of the relevant portion of the *Historia aurea* in "Appendix: John of Tynemouth's Account of the Siege of Jerusalem," in his "Alliterative Poetry in Old Jerusalem" (where a comparative English translation of the cannibalism episode is also available on 90–91). Hanna and Lawton make a detailed case for the poet's primary reliance on Josephus for this scene (xl–lii), while Galloway's essay argues that John of Tynemouth is the direct source.

2 For *The Golden Legend* version, see "In Context" section C.2.

3 The relevant Middle English text is printed, more extensively, at "In Context" section A.3.

places the reader into the scene, as if it is currently happening, is also the poet's choice, as is the dramatic placement of the episode at the end of a *passus* (a unit of the text readable in one sitting, similar to a chapter division). Though this is just one brief and oft-cited moment of the poem, it is a good example of how medieval authors, who valued creative reimagining and revision more than blunt originality, work with their sources. It also illustrates the transformative potential of translation and verse.

The suffering cannibalistic Jewish Mary is similarly elucidative of the *Siege* poet's ambivalent use of Christian tropes and Jewish history. As written first by Josephus, Mary is in some sense an authentic figure of Jewish history, but she is also a monstrous image of Jewish femininity that repeats the stereotyped and bigoted characterizations of other medieval texts.[1] She is, too, a sympathetic figure of sadness that betrays the cruelty and excess of the Romans, even as the poet argues that they justly avenge Christ—and she is a complex inversion of the Virgin Mary, who also sacrifices and consumes (via the Eucharist) her own child. These layers of meaning and signification are exploited by our poet. The cannibal Mary thus stands ultimately as an embodiment of the poem itself: a thing at once aggressive, violent, sympathetic, and vividly emotive, an artifact of firmly past religious and historical preoccupations, still accessible and painfully resonant.

The present volume provides for the first time a Modern English translation of the full text of *The Siege of Jerusalem*. The poem appears below in a prologue and series of six *passus* (Latin: steps) with varying numbers of quatrains. While some variation exists across manuscripts, this organization maintains the divisions and lineation of current Middle English editions. The subsequent "In Context" materials include excerpts from related texts and sources, along with samplings of the original Middle English and a bibliography to enable further reading and research.

---

1   See "In Context" sections D.2 and D.4 for examples. Several scholarly works on medieval Christian (gendered) ideas about Jews are also listed in the Works Cited and Recommended Reading list below.

Summary of *The Siege of Jerusalem*

The poem begins with the time and circumstances of Christ's death: he was crucified when Tiberius was the Roman emperor, when Herod Antipas ruled in Galilee, and under the direct authority of Pontius Pilate. The crucifixion was preceded by brutal torture, but Christ waited forty years to punish those who killed him. After this period of time, Titus and Vespasian enter the story: they are son and father, regional Roman authorities under Emperor Nero, and both suffer from horrible diseases. Titus has disfiguring growths on his face, and Vespasian is leprous and has wasps breeding in his nasal cavity. As Titus and Vespasian suffer, a sailor and merchant named Nathan is sent as a messenger from the Roman province of Syria, to report to Nero that Jews in his province are refusing to pay tribute to the emperor. On his way to Rome, he encounters a colossal storm that shipwrecks him on the shores of Bordeaux. Nathan is taken to Titus, who asks whether he knows how to cure his disease. Nathan responds by relating the basic tenets of Christianity and the story of the life and death of Jesus, and he also tells Titus about a healing cloth, owned by a woman named Veronica, that touched Christ's face and still retains Christ's image. Titus cries out in anger at Christ's death, and he is immediately healed of his disfigurement. He mourns Christ and vows to avenge his murder.

PASSUS 1 (lines 189–304)

Titus is baptized, and he and Nathan go to Rome to see Titus' father, Vespasian. Vespasian also confesses faith and vows to avenge Christ, and he verifies Nathan's story by speaking to the Pope, St. Peter. Roman "knights" are sent into Judea to seek tribute and retrieve the healing cloth from Veronica, and they return quickly, unable to secure tribute but with Veronica and her cloth in tow. St. Peter leads a celebratory procession through the streets. Along the way, Roman idols miraculously crumble, and sweet smells and bright light emit from the cloth. When Vespasian sees the image of Christ, he weeps. St. Peter touches him with the cloth, and Vespasian is immediately healed of his illnesses. At the same time, Nero is furious that the Jews continue to withhold his tribute, and he determines to take military action against them. A Roman council appoints Vespasian to lead the mission: he and his son Titus are deemed most appropriate to punish the Jews, since they are loyal to a man whom the Jews punished—and indeed we learn that they care most about avenging Christ, as they have already vowed to do. Military preparations are made at Rome, and the Roman fleet sails to the port of Jaffa. The poet curses Syria and Judean cities.

PASSUS 2 (lines 305–444)

The Roman army devastates Syria, and Jews all over the province flee to Jerusalem, where many are already gathered for Passover. The Romans advance and surround Jerusalem with an elaborate makeshift town and palisade, including an impressive command tent. Messengers from the city ask Vespasian's intentions, and Vespasian sends 12 men to threaten destruction unless the Jews surrender and turn over their high priest Caiaphas, who took part in Christ's condemnation. The Jews reject his commands and return his men humiliated. They propose to meet in armed battle the following morning. Enraged, Vespasian prepares for combat, hoists his imposing battle standard, and deploys his large army to posts around the city, including a vanguard of 16,000 led by Titus. The Jews inside Jerusalem also ready for battle. By dawn, both Romans and Jews are ready to fight in the Valley of Josaphat.

PASSUS 3 (lines 445–636)

The Jewish army exits the city in impressive numbers, with armored battle elephants and camels carrying men and gear. A lavish fortified elephant appears, carrying Caiaphas and many other Jewish men reciting Psalms and biblical passages. Vespasian gives a rousing motivational speech to his army and encourages them to forget their allegiance to Nero and serve Christ instead. Combat begins, described in gruesome detail by the poet, and the battle results in horrible losses for the Jews. Caiaphas and his men are captured as they try to retreat, and the Jewish army flees to the city, leaving the battlefield behind them covered in dead bodies. The Romans, however, have not suffered a single loss and remain refreshed and rested. The remaining Jews inside Jerusalem begin to defend the city walls with projectiles. At this, the Roman army withdraws for the night.

PASSUS 4 (lines 637–896)

At dawn the next day, the Romans clear away dead bodies, loot the battlefield, and begin a new attack on the city. Battle is now at the walls, which the Jews defend vigorously. The Romans, meanwhile, have completely encircled the city with battlements, so that no one can escape, and they begin to poison and block access to water supplies. Vespasian and Titus pronounce judgment on Caiaphas and his men and have them brutally tortured and executed. Vespasian orders the men's corpses to be burned and their ashes blown over the walls of the city. The second full day of combat comes to an end, as Vespasian worries about how to capture the city. The next morning, he arms himself and approaches the walls, taunting and threatening the city residents. From inside Jerusalem, a man called Josephus responds by trying to make the Romans believe the city has plenty of water—he hangs dripping wet laundry over the walls—but Vespasian recognizes the deception and renews the onslaught. The battle continues, and the Jews defend the city fiercely enough that the Romans are unable to capture it. Even Vespasian is wounded. The Romans withdraw, this time battle-worn and requiring doctors. In council the next morning, Titus proposes that they take the city by prolonged siege rather than by combat. All agree, and Vespasian suggests that they entertain themselves while they wait out the siege.

PASSUS 5 (lines 897–1112)

Back in Rome, Nero has been behaving badly. He has killed many people, including St. Peter and St. Paul. As a result, the Roman population turns on him, and he commits suicide. Several new emperors are chosen and killed in quick succession, until Vespasian, who we learn has held Jerusalem in siege for nearly two years now, receives word that the Roman senate has declared him emperor. Vespasian worries that returning to Rome to become emperor will mean abandoning his vow to avenge Christ, but his men agree that he can avenge by proxy, and that he should leave and put his son Titus in charge in his stead. When Titus hears that his father has indeed become emperor, he is so overjoyed that he becomes nearly paralyzed. The Romans seek a physician in Jerusalem, and Josephus comes to their aid. When Josephus' methods cure Titus, Titus offers wealth in return, but Josephus rejects the offer and returns to Jerusalem, where city residents are now suffering terribly from famine and disease. The passus concludes with the story of a woman so hungry that she eats her own child and the Jews' consequent decision that they must kill all noncombatants and negotiate terms. Titus refuses to negotiate, and the Jews begin to tunnel under the walls.

Passus 6 (lines 1113–1340)

As Titus rides around the city with only 60 men, the Jews ambush him and kill many of his entourage. Titus' brother Domitian, however, quickly arrives with reinforcements and kills the ambush party in short order. Titus offers a truce, which is now refused by the embittered Jews, and we learn that conditions in the city are deteriorating. The inhabitants are starving, disfigured, fighting for survival, and continually throwing the dead over the walls. Some do accept terms, but the Romans find that those who surrender are too ill to eat, because they have already eaten coins in an attempt to keep wealth from their enemies. The Romans therefore slaughter and loot the bodies of those who have surrendered, and the siege continues. Finally—after two full years now, says the poet—Titus once again attacks the city by combat. The Jews continue to fight, and even brutally kill one of Titus' most trusted soldiers, but eventually, after gory battle and miraculous portents, the Romans win. When Titus and his men enter the city, they are overwhelmed by the condition of the residents and the number of dead, but they proceed to loot and raze the Temple and city. Titus calls a slave market to sell the remaining Jews, and he sentences Pontius Pilate to life in prison, where Pilate commits suicide. The Roman army packs up and returns to Rome triumphant.

The Siege of Jerusalem

Prologue

In the time of Tiberius, Sir Caesar true,
The rightful emperor who ruled in Rome,
When Pilate was provost under that rich prince
And also judge of Jews in Judean lands,

Herod, under his rule, and by hereditary right,   5
Was called king of Galilee, when Christ died.
Though Caesar was spotless (he hated sin),
Through Pilate He was pained and put on the rood.[1]

A pillar was placed plain on the ground,
His body bound to it and beaten with scourges.   10
Whips of loose leather hit His white sides
Until He ran red with blood, as rain runs in the street.

Then strong men's hands set Him on a stool,
Blindfolded Him like a bee[2] and beat Him raw.
"If you are a prophet of price, prophesy!" they said.   15
"Which man among us walloped you last?"[3]

A tight thorn crown was thrust on His head.
They crowded Him with a cry and killed Him on a cross.
For all the harm He had, He was not in a hurry
To avenge the villainy of those who burst His veins.   20

---

1 *rood* Cross. The poet begins by recalling Christ's death, traditionally dated 33 CE.
    Tiberius ("Sir Caesar") was Roman emperor 14–37 CE, Pontius Pilate prefect of Judea
    26–36 CE, and Herod Antipas tetrarch of Galilee 4 BCE–39 CE. Cf. Luke 23.6–25.
2 *Blindfolded Him like a bee* The phrase "blind as a bee" is proverbial in the Middle
    Ages. Cf. modern "blind as a bat."
3 *If you are ... walloped you last* Cf. Matthew 26.67–68.

But He waited a while, in case they would convert,
Gave the guilty space, though it did little good—
Forty winters, as I find, and no fewer years—
Before princes pounced on those who wrought His pain, ·

25 Until the time came that Titus of Rome,
Who ruled all of Gascony and guarded Guyenne[1]
....
....[2]

A tribulation troubled him[3] then, in Nero's time.[4]
30 He had a severe sickness at the center of his face:
The lips lay in a clump, clotted on the cheek
Like an unclean tumor, clutched together.

A further wonder befell his fleshly father:
A nuisance of wasp-bees bred in his nose.
35 They hived in his head. He had had them since youth.
And he was called Vespasian, because of the wasp-bees.[5]

No sickness was worse than this man suffered.
He lay in a litter, a leper at Rome.

---

1   *Titus of Rome ... and guarded Guyenne*   Titus was emperor 79–81 CE. Before becom-
    ing emperor, he served under his father Vespasian in the First Jewish-Roman War and,
    after his father became emperor, led the siege and destruction of Jerusalem. His status
    as a vassal king of Guyenne and Gascony (southwest France) is legendary, found in the
    poet's sources.
2   ....   The text is corrupted here. Editors hypothesize that two lines are lost. See
    "In Context" section A.1 and its accompanying manuscript image for more informa-
    tion.
3   *him*   Titus.
4   *Nero's time*   Nero was emperor 54–68 CE. The 40-year time lapse mentioned in line
    23 is a traditional estimate, based on a calculation of the year of Jesus' death that
    lends biblical significance to the destruction of Jerusalem. The number 40 frequently
    marks important passages of time in the Bible (e.g., Genesis 7.12, Numbers 14.33–34,
    Matthew 4.2, Acts 1.3). For a late-medieval Jewish perspective on this dating, see "In
    Context" section D.5.
5   *he was called ... of the wasp-bees*   Vespasian was emperor 69–79 CE. Latin *vespa* means
    "wasp," but the fanciful etymology makes particular alliterative sense in the Middle
    English, where the name is spelled and pronounced "Waspasian." The physical dis-
    figurements, healings, and conversions of Titus and Vespasian are part of medieval
    legendary traditions associated with them. See for example "In Context" section C.2.

He was gone from Galatia, to gladden him briefly,
For he was king of that country, though afflicted so.[1]   40

No doctor living could relieve these lords,
No growing leaves[2] could heal their grim sores.
....
....[3]

Now, there was one Nathan of Greece, Nahum's son.[4]   45
He often sailed over the sea from city to city.
He knew many countries and many kingdoms,
Was a master mariner, and a merchant too.

Cestius sent him from Syria to Rome,[5]
To the noble emperor called Nero by name,   50
To make misfortune for him with a message from the Jews,
To tell of his tribute: that they would withhold it.

So Nathan took up his way toward Nero.
By the Greek lands and through grim waves,
He set his high sail over salt water,   55
Quickly with a dromond[6] drove over the deep.

Soon the sky waned and the sea grew dark.
Clouds bellowed above as if they would break.
A storm with red wind rose up around
And from the south side soon set on the sea.   60

---

1   *He lay in … though afflicted so*   I.e., Vespasian is in Rome, though he is a vassal king
    in Galatia (part of present-day Turkey), a legendary detail that the poet takes from his
    sources. Cf. "In Context" section C.2.
2   *growing leaves*   Medicinal plants.
3   ....   The text is corrupted here. Editors hypothesize that two lines are lost.
4   *Now, there was … Greece, Nahum's son*   The poem shifts scenes, to the adventures of
    a messenger on his way to Nero. The name "Nathan" suggests an early Christian of
    Jewish origin, only culturally Greek. Cf. the analogous characters and journeys at "In
    Context" sections C.1-2.
5   *Cestius sent him from Syria to Rome*   Gaius Cestius Gallus, Roman legate in the prov-
    ince of Syria (including Galilee and Judea) from 65?–67 CE.
6   *dromond*   Large, fast sea vessel.

It blustered over broad waters, burst forth hard.
Soon Nathan's vessel was knocked to the north.
Weather and the wind so clashed into waves
That what the captain commanded hurled into a heap.

65 Nathan went flat with fear, fell under the hatches,
Let weather and wind do as they wished.
The ship swerved aslant and shot far from Rome,
Toward unknown coasts, carried by waves,

Rapidly moving over rugged sea towers.
70 The broad sail burst suddenly in two,
So that one ship-end kept up toward heaven,
The other down deep as if it would drown.

Over wild waves he went, as if all would whirl forth,
Sailed through streams in the storms and the wind.
75 And at last with much misery, and as our Lord wished,
All was moved in a moment to the harbor of Bordeaux.[1]

By that bank people gathered, barons and knights,
And commoners too, and all considered it a marvel
That any barge or boat or breathing man
80 Had not perished there, as the perils were many.

They took him to Titus, for he knew the tongue,[2]
And he asked how far the flood had ferried him.
"Sir, I am come," he said, "from Syria
To Nero the sovereign at Rome, sent as a messenger

85 With certain letters from his servant Cestius,
Who is justice and judge of the Jewish laws.

---

1 *Over wild waves ... harbor of Bordeaux*   It is not realistic that a storm in the Mediter-
ranean would carry Nathan's ship to Bordeaux, but the poet marks this as miraculous
(i.e., it is "as our Lord wished") and is likely making a point of involving as much
of the Western world in the story as possible—specifically, known crusader routes to
Jerusalem.
2 *the tongue*   Probably Greek.

I would rather be in that land[1]—Lord, would that I were—
Than have all gold or goods that God ever made."

The king quickly called him into close counsel,
And said: "Do you know any cure or craft upon earth   90
To soothe the great sore that sits on my cheek?
I would right away reward you and send you to Rome."

Nathan answered him no, said he knew none:
"But were you, king, in the country where Christ died—
There is a worthy woman, a woman very pure,   95
Who has soothing and salve for every sore that is."

"The quicker you tell," Titus said, "the better for you:
What medicine is best that this maid makes,
Whether gums or grasses, or any good drinks?[2]
Or enchantments or charms? I charge you to say."   100

"None of those," said Nathan, "but I will tell you now:[3]
There was a man in our land, while He was living
Proven a prophet through praiseworthy deeds,
Born in a barn in Bethlehem, to a beautiful girl,

And she, a maiden unblemished whom man never marred,   105
As clean as a cliff from which crystals come forth,
Without help of any husband, save the Holy Spirit,
Conceived a king, a male child, by way of the ear.[4]

A token of the Trinity had touched her,
Three persons in one place, proven together: 110

---

1 *that land* Rome, where he should have landed if not for the storm.
2 *gums or grasses, or any good drinks* Medicinal salves, herbs, or mixtures.
3 *I will tell you now* Nathan here begins a 72-line history of the Christian church and
   its teachings that will culminate with a brief account of events following Jesus' death,
   including miraculous healings by Veronica's veil (lines 165–72).
4 *Without help ... of the ear* Medieval Annunciation iconography commonly depicted
   the Holy Spirit as a dove entering at the Virgin Mary's ear as the angel Gabriel an-
   nounced the pregnancy. Cf. Luke 1.28–38.

Each part is one God, and only one God all,
And all three are the one, as authorities[1] teach us.

The first is the Father, who was never created.
The second the Son, grown from His seed,
115   The third is the Holy Spirit, with them in Heaven,
Neither created nor made but conjointly proceeding.[2]

All are endless and equally one strength,
And were in essence endless before earth began.
The Son existed as soon as the Father himself;
120   The high Holy Ghost they had with them ever.

The second person, the Son, was sent to earth
To take fleshly form from a flawless maid.
Thus He came, concealed, to help us poor creatures,
And performed many miracles, until He suffered pain.

125   He turned water into wine with one word, first of all.
Ten lepers in one place He cured all at once.
Those pained with palsies He put to good health,
And raised dead men from death every day.[3]

Crooked and cancered, He cured them all,
130   Both the dumb and the deaf, with His dear words.
He did many more miracles than I can remember.
There is no clerk with counters who can count even half.

---

1   *authorities*   Church fathers, the elders of the Christian community.
2   *The third is ... but conjointly proceeding*   The Western Church's doctrine of the double procession of the Holy Spirit: the Spirit proceeds from both the father *and* the son rather than from the father *through* the son. This fine distinction in the nature of the Godhead remains a key point of doctrinal conflict between Eastern and Western Christianity.
3   *He turned water ... every day*   All miracles listed derive from the gospels. According to John 2.1–11, changing water into wine at the wedding in Cana was Jesus' first miracle. For others in this quatrain, cf. Luke 17.11–19, Matthew 9.1–8, and John 11.1–46 (although other gospel episodes are also relevant).

Five thousand folk—it is fantastic to hear—
He fed with two fish and five barley loaves,
So that each had his fill and yet more was left over,   135
Bits of bread and broken meat in twelve baskets full.[1]

There followed Him in one fellowship seventy-two
Chosen disciples to do what He deemed.
He sent them to cities to say all His teachings,
Always two by two, until they were separated.[2]   140

There followed Him, in another group, twelve good men,
Poor men and not proud—apostles they were called—
Whom He chose from the wretched to increase His church,
From the outcasts of this world, and these were their names:[3]

Peter, James, and John, and Jacob the fourth,   145
And the fifth of His fellows was one called Philip.
The sixth was called Simon, and the seventh next:
Bartholomew, who would not break His behest.

The eighth man was Matthew, who is much praised.
Then Thaddeus and Thomas—here are ten even—   150
And Andrew the eleventh, who put himself in peril
To preach before princes, was Peter's brother.

The last man was unfaithful, and foul in his deeds:
Judas, who sold Jesus Christ to the Jews.
He slew himself afterwards, in sorrow for that sin.   155
On a gallows tree his body burst at the belly.[4]

---

1 *Five thousand ... twelve baskets full* The miracle of the loaves and fish is recorded
   in all four gospels. John 6.9 supplies the "barley" detail, and all but Mark specify 12
   baskets. Note that the number 12 and its multiples feature prominently in the poem, a
   reflection of the biblical significance of the number (e.g., the 12 tribes of Israel, the 12
   apostles, and most importantly the description of the heavenly Jerusalem in Revelation
   21.10–14).
2 *There followed ... until they were separated* Cf. Luke 10.1.
3 *Poor men and ... were their names* Cf. Matthew 10.1–4, Mark 3.13–19, and Luke
   6.12–16.
4 *The last man ... at the belly* According to the gospels, Judas Iscariot sold Jesus to
   Jewish authorities for 30 pieces of silver and later hanged himself. Cf. Matthew 27.3–5
   and Acts 1.16–18.

After Christ had harrowed Hell and gone from here,[1]
They picked Matthias in place of that cursed man.
At that time both Barnabas and Paul were unbaptized
160 And knew nothing of Christ, but they came quickly after.[2]

Around Passover time, all the princes and prelates
Raged hot against Him for His holy works.[3]
It was a dreadful deed when they decided His death:
He was pained[4] through Pilate, the provost from Rome.

165 And that worthy woman, whom I mentioned before—
She is called Veronica and has His face on her veil,
So plainly portrayed that no point is lacking.
With love He left it for her, until her life's end.

There is no man in this world so miserably maimed,
170 By illness or ill-luck or by another mortal man,
Who kneels to that cloth and believes in Christ
And is not wholly healed at the wave of a hand."

"Ah, apostate Rome!" cried the king. "Ah, powerful emperor,
Caesar, you sinful soul who sent him[5] from Rome—
175 Why was your carcass not committed to dirt
When Pilate was placed to condemn such a prince?"

And before these words were come to an end,
The tumor the king had was entirely healed.
The face was faultless in flesh and in skin,
180 As fresh as features that have never been flawed.

---

1 *After Christ had ... gone from here* The apocryphal story of the "Harrowing of Hell"
   was extremely popular in the Middle Ages: it is the time, between the Crucifixion and
   Resurrection, when Christ went to Hell to declare victory over sin and to free righteous
   souls hitherto damned. Cf. Langland's *Piers Plowman* B text 18.
2 *They picked ... came quickly after* The poet completes the story of the election of the
   apostles before returning to the story of Jesus and his death in the next quatrain. Cf.
   Acts 1.20–26 (on Matthias), 4.36–37 (on Barnabas), and 9 (on Saul/Paul).
3 *Around Passover time ... His holy works* Cf. Luke 22.1–2 and Matthew 26.17–30.
4 *pained* Tortured, made to suffer (cf. line 8).
5 *him* Pontius Pilate, the appointed prefect of Judea.

"Ah, merciful Christ!" the king cried then.
"No work I have worked is worthy to tell you,
No deed I have done, God's dear Son,
But mourning your death without having seen you.[1]

And now: permit me my plea, blessed Lord,   185
To test Nero with trials and make new his sorrow.[2]
And I will ready myself to dole out destruction,
To put down those devils and avenge your death!"

Passus 1

"Tell me now," said Titus, "what token He left
To those who believed Him Christ and embraced His power?"   190
"Name the Trinity by name," said Nathan, "at once,
And be baptized besides, in blessed water!"

So they found a font-stone[3] and followed him there,
Made him a Christian king who would war for Christ.
Then messengers made their way to each shore   195
And brought all his baronage[4] to the port of Bordeaux.

Afterwards with Nathan he went into Rome
To show his father the fair and miraculous cure.
And he,[5] groaning gladly, thanked great God
And crying loudly to Christ exclaimed and said: 200

---

1 *Ah, merciful Christ ... having seen you*   Cf. the apostle Thomas in John 20.28–29.
2 *make new his sorrow*   Nero's first sorrow is loss of tribute from the Jews (see line 52).
3 *font-stone*   Stone basin used for baptism.
4 *baronage*   Typical medieval anachronism. The poet uses a term particular to English monarchal hierarchy to describe Titus' men. There are many such anachronisms throughout the poem, as in medieval romance generally.
5 *he*   Titus' father, Vespasian. There is quick movement between people and places in this passus that can make following the pronouns confusing: Titus gathers his retinue at Bordeaux and goes to Rome with Nathan (lines 195–98), where are Vespasian and the Pope and Nero (199–212); Roman knights journey to Judea and back (213–20); and eventually Titus and Vespasian take a fleet from Rome to Jaffa, near Jerusalem (281–96).

"Bold unblemished God, in whom I believe,
As you were born in Bethlehem of a beautiful maiden,
Send healing of my suffering, and I solemnly vow
To die for your death unless it is dearly repaid."

205 At that time Peter was Pope, and he preached in Rome[1]
The law and the doctrine that our belief demands.
Many folk followed him and turned to the faith,
And Christ through that man wrought many miracles.

Vespasian, who had the wasps, was aware of this.
210 He sent for him then, and he spoke the truth[2]
About Christ and the kerchief[3] that cured the sick,
Just as Nathan, Nahum's son who came to Nero, said.

Then knights of Rome were called into council,
And they quickly consented to send out couriers—
215 Twenty courteous knights to collect the kerchief—
And asked the emperor for safe conduct to accomplish the
    task.[4]

. . . .

---

1   *Peter was Pope ... preached in Rome*   Based on Matthew 16.17–19, Catholic tradi-
    tion holds that Jesus elected Peter to the first papacy. Apocryphal accounts of Peter's
    martyrdom at the direction of Nero, sometimes alongside St. Paul (see line 899), date
    his death c. 64–66 CE. Cf. the legendary account at "In Context" section C.3.
2   *He sent for him ... spoke the truth*   I.e., Vespasian sent for the Pope, and the Pope
    reported to Vespasian.
3   *kerchief*   Head covering, cloth; a frequent synonym for Veronica's veil.
4   *knights of Rome ... accomplish the task*   From here, the text is corrupted, and editors
    hypothesize that a significant number of lines are lost. The sense of this section of the
    poem, however, is that the Roman knights are sent to Judea on a joint political and re-
    ligious mission: to recover tribute from the Jews for Nero, and to retrieve St. Veronica's
    veil for Vespasian. Nero grants safe conduct for the political mission, which is unsuc-
    cessful. The pope meets the returning knights with a celebratory procession and grants
    them pardon (i.e., remission of sins) because their religious mission is successful: they
    return not only with the veil but also with Veronica herself. The conflicting objectives
    of the Roman empire and the Christian mission are a recurring issue in the poem. For
    an alternate version of how Veronica and her veil came to Rome, see "In Context"
    section C.1.

But without tribute or truce, and by troubled paths,
The knights came back very quickly, with the kerchief.
The Pope gave them pardon and came to them then
With a crowd of princes and dukes in procession.   220

When the woman who owned the cloth was aware
Of St. Peter the Pope, she dropped flat to the ground.
She embraced his feet and said to the man:
"Myself and this kerchief I commit to your keeping."

Then the man began to weep very bitterly   225
For the dreadful death of his dear master,
And he stood long in one spot before he could stop
When she uncovered the cloth that had touched Christ's body.

He accepted the cloth from the woman at last,
Received it with reverence and with running tears,   230
Moved quickly to the palace[1] with the crowd in tow,
And held it always up high so that all could behold.

Then the emperor bid twelve brave barons to go
And the Pope to depart from the people quickly.
Veronica with her veil and St. Peter the Pope   235
To Vespasian they brought, and presented them both.[2]

But a miracle happened amidst them all.
Fearful things transpired in their temple:
The Mahound and the mammets[3] crumbled to pieces
And collapsed as the cloth passed through the church.   240

---

1   *palace*   Nero's residence.
2   *the emperor bid ... presented them both*   I.e., Nero orders 12 Roman knights to take
    Veronica and Peter to Vespasian.
3   *The Mahound and the mammets*   False gods or idols, derived from Middle English
    versions of the name "Mohammed." The derivation is based on the wrongheaded
    medieval Christian conviction that Mohammed was a false god of the Muslims, but
    the words are used more generally here to describe statues of Roman gods. The word
    "church" in the next line is functioning similarly, referring to the Roman temple that
    the group passes through on their way to Vespasian, not to a place of worship specific
    to Christianity.

Then the Pope went into the palace[1] with the cloth.
Knights fell on their knees and venerated the veil.
A fragrance flowed from it. They all smelled it.
There was never sweeter odor nor air on earth.

245 The kerchief grew bright and began to beam
So that no man could behold it because of its light.
As it approached the prince,[2] he lifted his head.
For comfort from the cloth he cried out loudly:

"Behold, my lords, here is the likeness of Christ,
250 From whom I beg healing for His bitter wounds' sake."
There was weeping and woe and wringing of hands,
With loud sounds and sobs because of sorrow for Him.

The Pope lowered the veil and touched Vespasian's face,
Afterwards also his body all over. He blessed it three times.
255 The wasps went away—all sorrow went with them—
And what was leprous before was now unencumbered.

Then there was music and merriment, departing of strife.
They gave thanks to God, all those great lords.
The kerchief was carried from the crowd and hung high,
260 So common people could see it until supper time.

Vespasian called it the "Vernicle," after Veronica,
With gold and silver had it beautifully bedecked.
The face is still on the veil, just as Veronica brought it.
The Romans[3] have it in Rome and revere it as a relic.

---

1 *palace* Vespasian's residence now.
2 *the prince* Vespasian.
3 *Romans* Here simply people who live in Rome. Veronica's veil at Rome was a popular
pilgrimage destination in the Middle Ages, so much so that it became a stereotypical
emblem of the intrepid pilgrim, who might wear an image of the veil as a souvenir.
Cf. Chaucer's Pardoner in *The General Prologue* to *The Canterbury Tales* (line 687), and
Langland's palmer in *Piers Plowman* B text 5, 523–24. See the Introduction for more
information.

Meanwhile Nero was angry and had not a night's rest,   265
For his tribute was withheld, as Nathan had told.
He commanded his knights, earls and all men,
To come to hold council in the emperor's company.

The senators assembled immediately, with haste,
To determine who best could punish the Jews.   270
All adjudged by their judgment to dispatch those dukes
Who were cured by Christ whom they[1] killed on the Cross.

One of the two who took on the labor
Was Vespasian himself, and Titus the other,
A strong man on a steed and begotten of his body,   275
No less family to him than his own dear son—[2]

Crowned kings both and both much loved Christ,
Who had given them His grace and cured their afflictions.
Foremost in their hearts was to fulfill their vows
And to keep the contracts they had brokered before.[3]   280

Then was a rattling at Rome, polishing of mail-coats,
Summoning of soldiers, shields prepared.
They took leave of their lord,[4] lifted his standard—
A great dragon of gold—and all gathered set out.

By then ships were equipped, launched into the deep,   285
Tackled and attired, set onto tossing waves.
Fresh water and wine were hoisted on quickly,
And all sorts of supplies so that they would have strength.

---

1   *they*   The Jews. The logic here is that the Jews should be punished by those loyal to the
    man they punished.
2   *A strong man ... own dear son*   Description of Titus' military prowess and relationship
    to Vespasian.
3   *Foremost in their hearts ... had brokered before*   I.e., Titus' vow at lines 185–88 and
    Vespasian's at 201–04. The poet emphasizes their motivations in opposition to those of
    Nero, who just wants his tribute.
4   *their lord*   Vespasian, who is now commanding the legions headed to Syria. His battle
    standard is described in more detail at lines 389–416.

There were floines set afloat, and farcosts many,
290 Cogs and crayers, with battlements all,
Galleys[1] of great strength with golden banners,
Spread wide on the water about four miles around.

They drew up the topsail when tide demanded,
Had the wind at their back and left the seaboard,
295 Ventured over the waves with soldiers many,
And rejoined in port Jaffa, in Judean lands.[2]

Syria, land of Caesar, may you sigh forever.
May great sorrow be inflicted on your fine towns.
Cities under Zion, now your suffering is at hand:
300 The death of dear Christ shall be dearly avenged!

Now, Bethlehem, your boast is brought to an end,
Now Jerusalem and Jericho, condemned wretches you,
No king of your kind will be anointed with crown—[3]
For Jesus' sake shall no Jew rest in you more!

Passus 2

305 They set upon every section of Syria,
Despoiling and scorching all left behind.
Naught but smoke and lamenting endured in fine towns,
And red lashing flames all over the land.

---

1   *There were floines ... battlements all, / Galleys*   Specialized naval vocabulary. The poet
    is both answering the demands of alliteration and describing a full fleet: a *floine* is a
    small ship, a *farcost* a larger one, a *cog* a broad-based war ship, a *crayer* a small merchant
    vessel, and a *galley* a low sailing ship.
2   *port Jaffa, in Judean lands*   The port of Jaffa (part of present-day Tel Aviv) is one of
    the closest to Jerusalem and was a routine arrival port for pilgrims and crusaders in the
    Middle Ages.
3   *No king of ... anointed with crown*   Both a messianic assertion (i.e., no Jewish king
    need be anointed again because Jesus has already been anointed) and a political threat
    (i.e., there will be no more Herodian kings in power).

They took town and tower, a great many dwellings,
Burst through brass gates and won many cities, 310
The heathen host who remained, in fields or in towns,
Was wholly and horribly hewn to the ground.

The Jews flew to Jerusalem, where Josephus[1] lived—
Just how birds behave when a falcon will strike!
The city under Mount Zion sat very nobly, 315
A town guarded by many a turret and tower.

Princes and prelates and poor of the land,
Scholars and commoners from regions close by,
Were assembled at that city to make sacrifice
For Passover, as priests preached in their law.[2] 320

Many deceivers died at the swing of the sword,
For none went unharmed, even if he wanted to pay.[3]
But they put all to death and afterwards advanced
With engines[4] to Jerusalem, where Jews were thick.

They encircled the city with a resolute siege, 325
Set down large tents made of fine linens,
Raised them up quickly with ropes of rich silk,
Made a town of great tents from good Turkish cloth—

---

1   *Josephus*   Flavius Josephus (37–100? CE), Jewish historian of the First Jewish-Roman
    War and an eyewitness to the destruction of Jerusalem. He was a leader of Jewish forces
    at the siege of Jotapata (north of Jerusalem) in 67 CE, but he surrendered, curried favor
    with Titus and Vespasian, and received Roman citizenship. His works (originally writ-
    ten in Greek) are among the poet's sources. See the Introduction for more information,
    along with "In Context" section C.2, which includes an account of Josephus' surrender
    from a medieval Christian perspective.
2   *Passover, as priests preached in their law*   On the establishment of Passover, see Exodus
    12 and Numbers 28.16–25. The timing corresponds to the week of Christ's betrayal
    and crucifixion (see line 161). According to Josephus, the siege began 31 March 70 and
    lasted just over 140 days.
3   *Many deceivers died … wanted to pay*   I.e., even Jews who wanted to pay tribute were
    killed. The poet again highlights the conflicting motivations of Nero and his (now
    Christian) military leaders.
4   *engines*   Siege engines, large movable war machines.

Over the commander's they mounted a fine golden eagle,[1]
330 Gleaming, with four carbuncles,[2] on a gilded apple,
With large menacing dragons, all made of gold,
And beneath, likewise gilt, two lions reclining.

That pavilion was painted, hung with cloth all around,
Covered with histories in marvelous colors,
335 Coats of arms drawn—crenellations[3] above—
And a hundred rooms stood in that one spot alone.

At that point the tent was fortified with turrets,
Broad barriers were built, glorious to behold.
And when the siege was not yet fully accomplished,
340 From the city came messengers, sent from masters of law.[4]

They headed towards the highest commander,
Respectfully spoke their message at once,
Said: "The city has sent us to find your intent,
To hear why you have come, and what it is that you want."

345 Vespasian spoke not a word to those men
But sent messengers back, twelve strong knights,
Had them instructed to report to the men
That the cause of their coming was vengeance for Christ:

"Say I bid them be ready, the bishops[5] and others,
350 Before noon tomorrow, stark-naked all,

---

1 *golden eagle* The symbol of the Roman legion, augmented in the following lines
   with dragons and lions, symbols of power in medieval heraldry. From here, the poet
   describes the construction of Vespasian's large fortified command tent, including
   tapestries decorated with historical scenes and coats of arms (lines 333–35). Detailed
   descriptions of tents and battle standards are typical of medieval romance.
2 *carbuncles* Precious red stones, perhaps rubies or garnets.
3 *crenellations* Defensive battlements.
4 *masters of law* The Jewish leaders, here equated with masters or scholars of Jewish
   religious law.
5 *bishops* An anachronistic Christian term for the Jewish religious leaders, also com-
   mon in medieval Christian descriptions of Muslims (Saracens).

To give up their gates with rods[1] in their hands,
Each man in a white shirt and no other clothes.[2]

The Jews will take justice for Jesus Christ,
And bring out Caiaphas,[3] who betrayed Christ in council,
Or I will go to the walls and throw them all down.   355
No stone upon stone will stand when I'm done."[4]

These messengers[5] resolutely went to the city,
Where dwelled all the lords of the land who were left,
At once gave their account—pressed it aggressively—
Concerning Christ and Caiaphas and how they should come.[6]   360

And when the knights of Christ began to clamor,
The Jews took all twelve without further talk,
Bound their hands at their backs with wooden batons
And hacked off their hair and their blond beards too,

Stripped them naked as needles to the nether parts,   365
Blackened their faces with dusky dyestuff,
And then tied with a twine, to each knight's neck,
A cheese, and charged them to carry this to their chief:[7]

"Say we are unwilling to accept his commands,
Nor do we dread his judgment a whit. We intend his death.   370

---

1   *rods*   Or staffs, signs of office and authority. Cf. Genesis 38.18 and Numbers 17.1–5.
2   *Each man in ... no other clothes*   I.e., Vespasian commands the Jews to surrender in a
    particularly humiliating and submissive way.
3   *Caiaphas*   Jewish high priest who, according to gospel accounts, plotted against Jesus
    and took part in his trial. Cf. John 18.12–14 and Matthew 26.3–4, 57–66.
4   *No stone upon ... when I'm done*   An echo of Matthew 24.2, often repeated (see lines
    982, 1019–20, and 1289). The poet follows the gospels in viewing the destruction of
    Jerusalem as fulfillment of biblical prophecy (cf. Luke 19.42–44).
5   *These messengers*   Vespasian's knights now.
6   *how they should come*   I.e., Vespasian's instructions about how the Jews should come
    out from the city.
7   *Stripped them naked ... to their chief*   The humiliation of the knights is partly an
    inversion of Vespasian's demands, as they are aware (line 383): the Jews send back
    stripped-down Romans instead of Jews, tied with wooden rods rather than offering
    rods of authority. The rest is difficult to interpret: shaving and stripping have biblical
    parallel in 2 Samuel 10.4–5, but the significance of the blackening and the cheese is
    unclear.

He will find us on the battlefield—seek us no further—
Before prime[1] passes tomorrow—and tell your prince that."

The men hastened from the city, all twelve tightly tied,
To return the response made by the chief Jews.
375 Vespasian was never so livid as when those men arrived
Who were shorn and disgraced in so shameful a way.

These knights fell on knees in front of their king
And reported the tale just as it had happened:
"Of your threatening and intention they make only light.
380 We are bound for brazen speech and put out of clothes

In token of this truth: that they wish for battle
Before prime passes tomorrow—they delay no further.
What you intended will be turned back upon you.
Thus have they directed and deliver these cheeses."

385 Madly welling with wrath was Vespasian then.
He set a watch on the wall and quickly instructed
That all manner of men must on the morrow
Be assembled on the battlefield just after dawn.

He erected a siege tower in strong defiance,
390 Built it as a belfry[2] brimful with weapons.
When anything lacked for the folk in the field
At the belfry they would find the fix that they needed.

A gold dragon was hoisted and heaved up on high,[3]
Wide gaping as if he would swallow up men,
395 With mouth-arrows armed, and also a falchion[4]
Set under his feet, with four sharp blades.

---

1 *prime* First hour of the day, one of the prayer hours that structure the Christian
   liturgical day.
2 *belfry* Movable wooden siege tower, here used as a portable armory.
3 *A gold dragon ... up on high* I.e., Vespasian's battle standard, which the poet describes
   at length.
4 *falchion* Usually a broad sword, here an elaborate quadruple-bladed sword.

The points of the blades were pointed towards
The four parts of the proud world where they had waged war.
This falchion was set as a sign to the people:
The whole world they had won at the blade of the sword.   400

On a burnished-gold ball the beast had been mounted.
His tail wrapped around it so he could never turn
When lifted on high where the lord met his battle,
But always looked toward a land until it was taken.[1]

By this the city could see that no agreement would come,   405
No treaty about any truce, unless the town surrender
Or ride to battle the Romans, for they had taken their counsel[2]
To win the city by force or else be slain there.

Prepared to fly, his[3] broad wings were extended
With bells of bright silver all bordered about,   410
Ready to ring out loudly when anything moved,
With any gust of the wind that toward the wings blew.

The belfry was strongly blockaded then
With a terrible tower that loomed over the town.
Men might behold the beast by its brightness   415
From four miles away—the battlefields shone so!

On top of the tower high pennons[4] were placed,
Made of silk and sendal,[5] with silver embroidered,
Mixed with rich gold—like a coal-fire it glittered,
Or like sunbeams over the city, so all could see.   420

---

1 *His tail wrapped ... it was taken* I.e., the standard is constructed so that the dragon
   always faces the enemy.
2 *for they had taken their counsel* I.e., the Romans had taken the Jews' word (that they
   would be on the battlefield at dawn). But it is not obvious who is who. Both parties
   have threatened similarly, and the poet moves swiftly here between Roman and Jewish
   viewpoints and battle preparations.
3 *his* I.e., the golden dragon's (on the battle standard).
4 *pennons* Small flags, used to identify lords or men at arms.
5 *sendal* Fine, thin silk material.

In front of the four gates he[1] deployed sixty thousand
To persist for as long as the siege might last.
Watch was set on the walls so no one could escape.
Six thousand made a circle around the whole city.

425 That night there was nothing but the neighing of steeds,
Struggling into steel clothes and padding of helmets,
The arming of elephants and other slow beasts
With castles[2] on their backs to go against Christians.

Vespasian and all his men at dawn were arrayed
430 In steel clothes and came forth into the Valley
Of Josaphat,[3] where Jesus shall judge all things,
Formed firm battle lines and awaited those others.

First of all Titus took control of the vanguard,
With sixteen thousand soldiers assigned, to be sure,
435 And as many in the mid-guard were marked to remain
Where Vespasian was, amidst dukes and princes.

And sixteen thousand were in the third guard as well,
With Sir Sabin of Syria,[4] a strong and excellent knight,

---

1 *he* Vespasian. The end of this passus describes his impressively large army, but Jews
   will dramatically outnumber Romans. Similarly uneven estimates were used by cru-
   sade chroniclers to emphasize miraculous victories. Cf. the selection from Raymond
   d'Aguilers at "In Context" section D.1c.

2 *castles* Structures built onto the backs of large animals to hold men and weapons.
   This quatrain describes the late-night preparations of the Jews, and the exotic war-
   beasts here and elsewhere mark them as stereotypically Eastern. The use of armed ele-
   phants in battle has biblical parallel in 1 Maccabees 6.28–46 (where they are used by
   the Greco-Syrian army), and many legendary, romantic, and historical parallels exist
   in medieval accounts of Alexander the Great and crusade battles. Cf. "In Context"
   sections B.1 and D.1c.

3 *Valley / Of Josaphat* Location of the Last Judgment according to Joel 3.1–2 (Hebrew
   Yehoshafat means "God has judged"), traditionally associated with the Cedron valley
   and accepted by medieval Christians as the likely site of Christ's return.

4 *Sir Sabin of Syria* Identity uncertain. Josephus mentions a Roman tribune prominent
   in the siege of Jotapata by this name, but the poet describes here a mercenary leader who
   provides an additional 4,000 Syrian men for the Romans (line 440).

Who was prince of that province and ruled many people,
Forty hundred in his army with helmets to show.   440

And ten thousand stayed near the tent at the rear,
To keep horses from harm, and their harnesses too.
And at that, booming trumpets blared from the city
And banner-bearers appeared—now bless us, our Lord!

Passus 3

The Jews soon assembled and came from the city,   445
A hundred thousand on horses, in hauberks[1] attired,
Not counting the foot soldiers at the four gates
Who pressed to the field with large shields in hand.

Five and twenty elephants came out from the town,
Beasts of defense with broad castles on their backs.   450
And on each of the elephants were many armed men,
A hundred at all times housed within wooden structures.

Then dromedaries[2] advanced, devilishly thick,
A hundred with leg armors and harnesses of mail.
Each beast held a big tower wherein were strong men: 455
An even twenty in each tower reckoned by tally.

Steel-clothed camels came forward then,
Moved quickly to the field—an amazing number
Hastened to battle—and each had on its back
A wooden turret full with ten armed men.   460

There was a wondrous number—whoever wished to know—
Of chariots full of choice men, charged with weapons.
That day many brave men, who had never been fearful,
Were found dead in the field by the time the fight ended.

---

1 *hauberks* Coats of chain mail or plate armor.
2 *dromedaries* Camels, apparently distinct from those in the next quatrain.

465 A single armed elephant came out last,
Carrying a castle that was skillfully made.
A tabernacle in the tower[1] was richly attired,
Set up like a pavilion on pillars of silver.

A chest of white silver rolled about within
470 On four golden posts that held it up from the floor,[2]
Near an excellent chair and twelve candlesticks
Of inlaid burnished gold, with candles bright burning.

Fine carbuncles were on the sides of that seat,
Where sat Caiaphas, clad in rich cloth.
475 A plate of gleaming gold was set on his breast,
With many precious pearls and polished cut stones.[3]

Learned men of the law[4] who well could sing loudly
Sat beside him with Psalters and recited the Psalms
Of brave King David and other dear histories
480 Of Joshua the noble Jew, and of Judas the knight.[5]

---

1   *tabernacle in the tower*   Canopied dais within the wooden structure, where *tower* is likely an alliterative synonym for *castle* in the previous line.

2   *chest of white ... from the floor*   The chest may be the Ark of the Covenant (described in Exodus 25.10–39), but the rich trappings of this elephant may also allude more generally to 1 Maccabees 6.43. The poet uses the battle scene in 1 Maccabees 6 extensively, but his doing so inverts the biblical narrative, wherein the Maccabees (Jews) are heroically fighting to regain Jerusalem from villainous Greco-Syrian forces that outnumber them and attack them with war elephants. In reciting the story of Judas Maccabeus below ("Judas the knight" in lines 479–80), the Jews may therefore be reciting an inversion of the battle enacted in the poem. Cf. "In Context" section B.1.

3   *Where sat Caiaphas ... polished cut stones*   Caiaphas' clothing reflects biblical description of Israelite priests, specifically the ephod (sleeveless garment) and breastplate described in Exodus 28.6–30.

4   *Learned men of the law*   Scholars of Mosaic law.

5   *King David ... Joshua ... Judas the knight*   The three Jewish "worthies" (among a group of nine that includes pagans and Christians) identified in the Middle Ages as model heroic and chivalrous warriors. "Judas the knight" is Judas Maccabeus, not to be confused with Judas Iscariot. Whether "of brave King David" refers to the authorship of the recited Psalms or to the content of the "dear histories" (or both) is unclear. Psalm books existed for Christians and Jews ("Psalters" or "Tehillim"), and, in both Christian and Jewish traditions, King David is the author of the Psalms *and* the subject of the books of Samuel. In the medieval Old Testament canon, Joshua and Maccabees are the first and last of the historical books of the Bible, but the books of Samuel are among the histories as well.

Caiaphas himself took a roll[1] from the chest
And read how the people ran through the red waters
When Pharoah and his forces were drowned in the flood,
And much of Moses' law he pronounced at that time.

When this faithless people advanced to the field   485
And formed battle lines there, with many brave men,
Because of the banners, vanguard horns, and armed beasts,
No man through the multitude could see to the city.

Vespasian surveys the valley all around,[2]
Covered over with banners up to the town gates.   490
To the barons and brave men there all around him,
He says: "Lords in this land, listen to my speech:

There is neither king nor knight come to this place,
Baron nor bachelor,[3] nor anyone who follows me,
Whose reason for coming is not vengeance for Christ   495
Upon this faithless people who deceitfully slew Him.

Look to the mocking and to the hard wounds,
To the binding and the beating He took on His body—
Let not this lawless people ever laugh at His harms,
He who bought us from sin with the blood of His heart!   500

I quitclaim[4] the quarrels of all living men
And the claims of every king, save Christ alone,

---

1   *roll* Scroll. The detail suggests that Caiaphas reads from a Torah scroll, which would
    include the story of the exodus from Egypt and the parting of the Red Sea (see Exodus
    13–14).
2   *Vespasian surveys the valley all around* From here, the poet often uses the historic
    present tense to place the reader in the center of the action. As is common in Middle
    English narration, however, he moves freely between the past tense and the historic
    present—more often than can be smoothly represented in Modern English translation.
3   *bachelor* Young knight, or a knight of low rank.
4   *quitclaim* Formally renounce or release, give up claim to. Vespasian here legally re-
    leases his men from all obligations of service to any superior (other than Christ) and
    specifically from any obligation to secure tribute for Nero. The only relevant injustice
    or breach is the one that pertains to Christ. On his reasoning, see Matthew 6.24, Luke
    16.13, and Mark 12.13–15.

On whom this people had no pity while torturing,
As His passion proves, if one reads the Paschal story.[1]

505 It matters not at this moment to remember Nero,
Nor to negotiate any truce for the tribute he demands:
Whether he likes it or no, I quitclaim his quarrel
With these rebels to Rome and want only justice for wrong.

For today a greater matter we recall to our minds:
510 That with justice royal prerogative falls unto Rome—[2]
The might and the strength both, the mastery and more,
The lordship over every land that lies under Heaven.

Permit this faithless people to win from us in battle
Not a horse or a harness unless they buy it hard,
515 Not a plate nor pisane,[3] not a bauble off a pendant
So long as we have limbs and any life left!

For they are spineless in a fight, and false of belief,
And think they can kill the whole world with one blow,
Neither grounded in God nor trusting in grace—
520 But all in the savagery of battle and in strength alone.

And we are summoned to serve the Lord today—
Now high Heaven-King, take care of your own!"
The men kneel down before him and all say aloud:
"Anyone who deserts today, the Devil take his soul!"

525 The horns sound at once, horses draw near,
Steeds stomp in the field under padded steel,

---

1   *Paschal story*   Easter story, including the suffering and death (passion) of Christ. The
    poet's Middle English word for the term is *paas*, which may also be related to the Latin
    passus (step) and can refer to a biblical passage or to the divisions of an alliterative
    poem, like this one. Cf. "In Context" sections B.5-6.
2   *That with justice ... falls unto Rome*   I.e., Rome justly has a right to exert imperial
    influence. Since Vespasian negates the legal rights of the emperor in favor of loyalty to
    Christ, this claim also alludes to the papacy.
3   *Not a plate nor pisane*   Not a breastplate, nor the chain-mail that protects the neck and
    upper torso.

Sturdy men mount them, step into stirrups,
Knights cross themselves and take hold of their helmets.

With loud clarion call and with cornemuse pipes,
The timbrels and tambours[1] now loudly intone   530
And make shrieking roar—and the Jews shrink back,
Like women who writhe in a swoon as childbirth approaches.

They take up lances at once, leap forward as one—
They moved with the force of a flash from a flint-stone.
Dust was kicked up high and all things grew dark,   535
As when thunder and thick rain are shaking the skies.

They stab through the men—their lances broke—
And knights crash down onto cold earth.
They fought hard in the field, and ever beneath them
The false,[2] without words, were swooning to death.   540

Titus turns to charge, brings down the best,
Unhorses the mightiest in hostile engagement,
Then with a bright blade beats one so hard
That the brain and the blood slop onto the field.[3]

He went through another flank with a hard weapon,   545
Struck with bright steel while the blade lasted—
On high he brandishes his blade, looks like a boar![4]
He hacked them down violently, took whomever he could.

From the golden gear and the precious stones
The field was lit up like the beams of the sun.   550
For the shimmering of shields and the shining of helms,
It looked like the firmament was burning in fire.

---

1 *cornemuse pipes, / The timbrels and tambours* Horn pipes or bagpipes, tambourines,
   drums.
2 *The false* The Jews.
3 *Titus turns ... onto the field* The poet zooms in on Titus and his battle skills. Although
   we have seen little of him since Vespasian's healing, he will eventually lead the Roman
   army and take charge of the siege.
4 *He went through ... like a boar* The warrior-boar comparison is proverbial in the
   Middle Ages. Cf. line 785.

Vespasian observes the vanguard in the valley,
How the heathen army still holds its ground.
555 He had come with a fine army to battle the false:
They strike hard in unison, like griffins[1] enraged.

Hastily their spears turned into splinters,
Shields on their shoulders split into firewood.
They shook out of sheaths what was well sharpened[2]
560 And pounded the metal through merciless hearts.

They hacked down the heathen, charged forward together,
Sheared apart golden armor, shattered coats of mail.
Streams swelled with blood all over the valley,
And gushes from golden clothes ran as from gutters.[3]

565 Meanwhile Sir Sabin puts himself in position,
Rides up with the rear guard and follows the troops—
He moved in to attack most fiercely those castles
That beasts had borne on their backs out of the town.

He takes aim at the elephants, which were so abhorrent,
570 And cuts out the entrails with well-sharpened spears:[4]
Intestines burst forth so that a hundred ground-clearers
Would be hard-pressed to bury what remained on the field.

Castles clatter to the ground, camels burst open,[5]
Dromedaries meet with their death very quickly—
575 The blood foamed from them into great motionless pools,
So that steeds were knee-deep as they dashed through the
    valley.

---

1 *griffins* Legendary beasts with the body of a lion and the head and wings of an eagle
   or large bird.
2 *what was well sharpened* Swords.
3 *And gushes ... as from gutters* I.e., gushing blood flowed from wounds, soaking
   through armor as plentifully as water from rain gutters. Cf. the poet's description of
   the bleeding Christ at line 12.
4 *He takes aim ... well-sharpened spears* Cf. 1 Maccabees 6.43–47, where the hero who
   takes down the elephant is a Jew (the brother of Judas Maccabeus).
5 *camels burst open* Under the pressure of falling men and castles, or by Sir Sabin's
   method, described in the previous quatrain.

The men who were in the wooden structures on top,
As those defenses and the hard earth hurtled together,
Became utterly blind from the dust and the noise,
Were all smothered in steel, completely cut off,   580

And beneath fallen dromedaries they died on the spot.
There was none left alive even able to stand,
Save one single elephant there at the great gate,
Where Caiaphas the clerk[1] rides in his castle.

He sees the destruction wrought and retreats   585
With twelve other masters[2] of Moses' law.
A hundred helmeted men chase them in haste—
And they captured them before they could exit the castle.

They bound the bishop[3] in so vile a way
That blood burst out from under each binding,   590
And they brought all the beaux-clerks[4] up to the belfry,
Where the battle standard stood, and positioned them there.

With the bishop they brought (though it tormented him)
The beast and the castle and all the bright gear,
The chair and the candleholders and the carbuncle stones,   595
The scrolls that they read from and all precious books.

It was then that those faithless people lost heart.
They turned back to the town, with Titus pursuing.
He left many from the false army lying in the field:
A hundred in their helmets downed by his hand alone.   600

---

1 *clerk* Word that denotes multiple professions and credentials in Middle English.
   It can mean cleric or clergyman, scholar or writer or student (especially university
   student), or a keeper of records or accounts. The first is probably most relevant to
   Caiaphas, but the poet uses the word to describe many people—notably only Jews,
   with the possible exception of line 132.
2 *masters* Scholars, apparently the same as the "learned men" at line 477.
3 *bishop* Caiaphas, an anachronistic Christianization used several times for the Jewish
   high priest.
4 *beaux-clerks* Fine or excellent scholars, a French-English compound, used elsewhere
   in Middle English texts only as an epithet for the Anglo-Norman King Henry I.

The false Jews in the field are fallen as thick
As hail from heaven, in heaps upon heaps.
So covered was the field, all the broad valley,
With the bodies of the dead, drenched in blood,

605 That no steed could step unless on steel clothes,[1]
Or on a man, or on a beast, or on shining shields.
So great was the multitude that remained on the earth
Where so many were wounded—and a wonder if not!

Yet the Romans were as rested as if fresh from Rome,
610 Each man unharmed and not a bauble broken.
Not a tip of a piece of prized armor was pierced.
Until compline[2] time Christ protected His knights.

One hundred thousand helmets on the heathen side
Were fallen dead in the field before the fight ended.
615 Only seven thousand survived, and they flew to the city,
Secured the walls with great sorrow and held on within.

At once men rush forward to fasten the gates,
Bolt them up firmly with big iron bars,
Tug up the drawbridges with twisted-link chains,
620 And put each portcullis to the ground with a pin.[3]

Valiantly they determine to defend the walls
With fresh, untried troops—and they made a great stand!
They haul into towers barrels full of boulders,
Large hunks of grey marble and heavy sandstone.

625 Bravely they fought, casting stones from on high,
Shooting out quarrels[4] from crossbows at once.

---

1 *steel clothes* Armor, i.e., the dead bodies still wearing their armor.
2 *compline* Night, the last prayer hour of the Christian liturgical day. Cf. the poet's uses of the morning prayer hour "prime" at lines 372, 382, and 708.
3 *portcullis ... with a pin* I.e., they secure the heavy metal grating that blocks the city gates. The pin is either in the lowering or locking mechanism (a pin in the wheel, or a pin that fixes the portcullis to the ground).
4 *quarrels* Heavy arrows.

That other people below attacked them again,
Until all the broad valley was dampened with dew.[1]

The dukes and the rest withdrew from the ditch—
The stones from the walls had become so deadly—   630
Followed their king, as clean as when they came.
Not a man had a mark, and they lost not a one.

Princes move swiftly toward their great tents,
Unarm themselves quickly and rest all the night,
With a watch on the walls. To many men's sorrow,   635
They will not let the heathens remain so unharmed.

Passus 4

Right as the red dawn rose in the sky,
Trumpets blew widely to make the men rise.
The king commanded with a cry what soon began:
Strip bare the battlefield of all dead bodies,   640

Despoil the slain folk—none should spare them—
Get belts and gear, gold and good gems,
Bracelets, bright brooches, rich bezants,[2]
Helmets made of gold, and magnificent hauberks.

They tossed dead upon dead—it was dreadful to see—   645
Made wide paths in this way and went to the walls.
They assembled at the city to start the assault,
Thick groups of people positioned at the four gates.

They brought the wooden towers that they had taken
And set them up tall, right against each gate.   650

---

1   *That other … dampened with dew*   I.e., the Romans, from the foot of the walls, con-
    tinued to attack until nightfall.
2   *bezants*   Gold coins.

With the biggest they began to erect a siege tower,
Built it up from the ground on twelve large posts.[1]

It was built up so high and marvelously wide
That five hundred at once could fight at the walls.
655 Valiant men rushed up the stairs, ran to the top,
And started with an onslaught to torment the city.

Quarrels flaming with fire shot out hard,
And arrows flew swiftly, with poison envenomed,
Aimed at city towers, attacking the Jews—
660 Through battlements many brave men met their death.

They struck down and burnt very strong buildings,
Burst through the barricades and the broad towers.
Like this many brave men were ready to battle,
Prepared for a long war around the wide walls,

665 Which were big and broad and difficult to win,
Wondrously high to behold, open trenches beneath
With embankments built up high on both sides—
Plain dangerous to win, except by shrewd tricks.[2]

Archers in the trenches aimed high their weapons,
670 Shot sharply upwards toward those fair walls
With arrows and crossbows and all that could harm,
To frighten the people who made their defense.

The Jews defended the walls with no lack of tricks:
They threw onto the people hot boiling pitch,
675 Hurled down many barrels full of brimstone and lead,
Poured out hot liquid like clear gleaming water.

---

1 *the wooden towers ... twelve large posts* The Jewish spoils of war are used against Je-
   rusalem: these are the fortifications seized from the war beasts of Caiaphas and his
   men. The largest structure (i.e., Caiaphas') serves as the foundation for a particularly
   imposing Roman siege tower.
2 *Which were big ... by shrewd tricks* Described like a typical medieval castle or forti-
   fied city, Jerusalem is surrounded by a large stone wall, with many towers and turrets
   and crenellations, gated with drawbridges and portcullises, and surrounded by deep
   trenches and a moat (these may be the same, as moats could be filled with water or
   not). Cf. the description of the city at "In Context" section D.1c.

Vespasian veers from the walls, cursing them all.
Still others made ready and prepared the siege engines,
Shot up at the ramparts and overfull turrets,
Smashed to the ground many dear days' work.   680

By then men had made a great strong palisade[1]
That surrounded the city with many tall towers,
So that no man might circle it without using wings,
Nor could anyone under the sun leave the city.

Then they fill up the trenches with the dead bodies,   685
Cram them with carrion, under the ramparts,
So the stink of the vapor will strike over the walls
To infect the cursed people who wanted to keep them.[2]

They stop up the water that runs to the town—
Every little stream where any trickle flowed—   690
With sticks and with stones and with stinking beasts,
So the people enclosed could control no more water.

Vespasian returns to his tent, with Titus and others,
Calls a council at once to set judgment on Caiaphas,
To say with what death he should die by their counsel,   695
Along with the learned clerks they had captured.

Judges upon their dais judge swiftly
That each man be flayed alive, the flesh clean off,
First dragged behind horses across a wide field,
And then as a group be hung on high gallows   700

With feet facing the sky for all people to see,
Anointed with honey on each hideless side,
Four stray dogs and cats with sharp claws
Bound up and tied tight to Caiaphas' thighs,

---

1 *palisade* Fortified enclosure. The Romans have wholly encircled the city with elabo-
   rate quickly-made ramparts and siege towers. The enclosure is also a fulfillment of
   Jesus' prophecy in Luke 19.41–44.
2 *them* Walls. The sense here is that the rotting corpses will contaminate supplies and
   sicken the Jews—a kind of germ warfare.

705 Two apes at his arms, to torture him more,
So they shred up the raw flesh into red pieces.
Thus he was tortured and pierced in his sides
From prime until sundown, and in summer time.[1]

The learned men of the law, just a little beneath,[2]
710 Were tormented on a tree, hung upside down.[3]
Two vicious dogs were tied tight to each clerk.
The whole city could see the sorrow they suffered.

Jews jumped from the walls for woe at that time.
Seven hundred slew themselves in sorrow for their clerks.
715 Some grasped their own hair and pulled it from their heads,
And some for their grief dashed themselves against ground.

And when they were dead the king had them undone[4]
And bade: "Build a bale-fire to burn up the corpses.
Cast Caiaphas therein, and all his clerks too,
720 And burn every bone right down to brown ashes.

Then go to the wall on the windiest side
And let that powder blow broadly across the whole city.
'Here is dust for your drink!' cry down to them then.
Bid them swallow that broth for the soul of their bishop."

725 Thus ended cursed Caiaphas and his twelve clerks,
All mangled by beasts and burned up in the end,

---

1 *From prime until ... in summer time*   According to the poem, this is only the second
day of a siege that began around Passover (late March in 70 CE). The word "summer,"
however, may refer generally to the warmer half of the year and serves to emphasize
that Caiaphas hung for a very long time.

2 *just a little beneath*   I.e., positioned just below Caiaphas.

3 *Were tormented on ... hung upside down*   The spectacular public punishment of Caia-
phas and his men is also a grotesque inversion of the torture of Christ: the upside-down
hanging and Caiaphas' pierced sides most clearly connect the cases. There may also be
a connection to the death of St. Peter (lines 898–99), who tradition holds was killed by
inverted crucifixion. Cf. "In Context" section C.3.

4 *And when they ... had them undone*   I.e., Vespasian had the dead bodies of Caiaphas
and his clerks removed from their gallows.

In token of the treason and pain they had wrought
When Christ through their counsel was driven to His death.

By then day was done, and the skies had dimmed.
The moors and the mountains darkened all around.   730
Birds came to the earth and rustled their feathers.
The night watch moved to the wall, watchmen to signals.

Bright fires are kindled far and wide through the army.
The king and his council speak in confidence together.
They choose commanders[1] and then quarrel no more,   735
Appoint a watch against assaults—and then they went to bed,

Both the lords and their knights went to get rest.
Vespasian lies in his tent. He sleeps very little.
Instead he moans and he turns and he tosses about,
Often wrenches with worry and thinks about the city.   740

When shadows and the shining day split in two,[2]
And the larks on high lift up their voices,
Men lift themselves out of bed with the loud trumpet call
Blowing both on the battlefield and on the town walls.

Vespasian rises from bed, readies himself well,   745
In fine golden clothes from the face to the crotch.[3]
Over clothes of fine cloth the prince first places
A thick-braided mail coat and then a breastplate

With a lance-rest of grey steel mixed with fine gold.
Over this he puts a cloak decorated with his arms.   750
A great girdle of gold, and no other gear,
He lays about his loins with strong fastening loops.

---

1   *commanders*   Night commanders, to supervise the watch.
2   *When shadows and ... split in two*   I.e., when dawn breaks.
3   *In fine golden ... to the crotch*   The arming of Vespasian—albeit with a focus on the
    loins, torso, and head—is an example of a popular medieval romance formula. Cf. the
    arming of Gawain in *Sir Gawain and the Green Knight*, 2.566–669 and 4.2009–46.

A bright burnished sword he ties just above,
With a hilt and a pommel of pure polished gold.
755 A wide shining shield he hangs at his shoulder,
Buckled at the neck with bright gold and set above

Gauntlets of grey steel, which were lined with gold.
He picks up his harness, and he calls for his horse.
He buckles up quickly his fine golden helmet,
760 Fashioned with a visor and mouthpiece, no less.

Encircling the top was a crown of pure gold,
Wrapped around the helmet, full of precious stones,
Set proudly with pearls inlaid at perfect peaks,
And likewise with sapphires all over the sides.

765 On a strong steed he strides, gallops into the field,
Swift as a lion loosed from its chains.
His men saw him then, and each said to the other:
"This is a worthy king to command men at arms!"

He turns at the brass gates before he comes to a stop
770 And beats on them with his sword so the metal rings out:
"Come forth, you wretches, you who murdered Christ,
Accept Him as your king—before you get some more!

Observe from the walls what sorrow is at hand.
Though you are starving, may you find no more food.
775 Though you go waterless, may you never win a drop,
Even if it means death and the end of your days!

The big palisade I have built near the trenches
Has enclosed the whole town—and who can cross it?
Here forty men can defend against five hundred.
780 Even if you were giants, you would have to stay back!

A more valorous maneuver would be to beg mercy
Rather than perish, foodless, where no power helps."

No one says a word, but all watch for their chance
To slay with stiff stones any man who might stray.[1]

Then, like a wild boar enraged, he yanks at his bridle: 785
"If you want to die like dogs, the Devil take who cares!
But before I turn from this wall, you will speak words—
And reply wisely, or I won't acknowledge your talk!"

By that time, a Jew—the crafty Josephus—[2]
When water was wanting had concocted a trick: 790
He had woolen clothes plunged into water
And hung on the wall, as if they'd been washed.

The clothes dripped down, dried very quickly.
Steam rises from them. The Romans look on,
Conclude that the clothes have had a good washing,   795
That no one in the place can be without water.

But Vespasian sees the trick well enough,
Laughs loudly at it and directs his lords:
"Do not be downcast, though they make this boast.
It is only war tricks, for they do lack water!"   800

Then nothing was left but to renew the labor,
To attack the city on both sides with separated flanks.
With magonels[3] they struck with immeasurable blows,
And much masons' labor[4] they ruined at that time.

---

1   *No one says … who might stray*   I.e., the Jews make no response but hold position and
    watch for a chance to kill wandering Romans.
2   *Josephus*   Many of the events associated with Josephus in what follows are taken from
    historical accounts of the siege of Jotapata, where he was a leader of Jewish forces in 67
    CE.
3   *magonels*   Siege engines used for throwing stones. This phase of the battle is focused
    on projectiles and their effects: all war machines and combat maneuvers in the rest of
    the passus are of this kind. Cf. the crusader siege of Jerusalem at "In Context" section
    D.1c.
4   *masons' labor*   Stone walls and fortifications built by masons.

805 Josephus was aware of this—he knew much of war—
And he set on the wall-sides, where the stones hit,
Sacks full of chaff to offset the strokes
So they did little damage, just made a big din.

The Romans rush forward and tie onto poles
810 Scythes for the sacks, spectacularly sharp,
To cut at the ropes and slice sacks apart,
So that all falls flat, drops down to the moat.

But the crafty Josephus burned all their engines
With hot burning oil, and he caused great harm:
815 Vespasian was wounded there, very severely,
With a hand-dart driven through the hard part of his heel.

It penetrated the boot and pierced through the bone
Of his leather-wrapped foot, to the side of his steed.[1]
Men rushed to him rapidly, a group one hundred strong
820 Who would avenge that wound or suffer in sorrow.

They fixed on the barricades, eagerly aimed,
Fought very fiercely, thrust hard with spears.
They strike and kill Jews—and by then many engines
Were prepared on the field to take aim at the town.

825 Marvels were seen there, as men may hear tell:
A man's brain was split open with one brutal stone.
That pebble sent the largest piece of the skull
A furlong or more, flying into the field.

A woman heavy with child was hit on the womb
830 With a stone from a ladder,[2] as the story goes,
So the baby was hurled clean away from the body
And was sent like a ball over the city walls.

---

1 *his leather-wrapped foot … of his steed* I.e., the dart went completely through Vespasian's foot and into the horse he was riding.
2 *from a ladder* Thrown from a ladder.

Many men were brained and bruised to death,
Women split open beneath thrown down stones.
Strongholds were pierced from the roof to the floor   835
And with many turrets fell down near the Temple.[1]

The city would have been taken right then by attack[2]
Had they not been so fierce—those fiend-serving people
Who assaulted the Christians and defended the walls
With arrows and crossbows and catapults many,   840

With spears and projectiles hurled out hard,
With darts driven downward, causing deep wounds,
So that many men from Rome, by the time the sun set,
Would much rather a doctor than any war games!

Vespasian puts a stop to the battle, relieves men   845
Who were beaten bloody beneath their bright iron.
They turn to their tents with what troubles they have,
Weary of that work and grievously wounded.

Helmets and hauberks they quickly remove.
Doctors by torchlight tend to their sores,   850
Wash wounds with wine and bandage with wool
And with chrisms and prayers prescribed within charms.[3]

Afterwards every man went to his meal.
Though they were wounded, no woe was mentioned,
No grief, but rather dancing and dinning of pipes   855
And a drummer's loud beat all through the night.

---

1   *the Temple*   This is the first mention of the Temple in the poem, an indication that
    the Romans are moving closer to the center of Jerusalem and to the religious goals and
    prophetic fulfillments of the siege.
2   *The city would ... then by attack*   I.e., by combat alone, as opposed to a prolonged
    siege.
3   *chrisms and prayers prescribed within charms*   Medicinal oils and charms. The charms
    may be protective prayers or amulets containing written prayers and medicinal recipes.
    Cf. Titus' expectations of Veronica's healing abilities at lines 97–100.

When the dark receded and the day burst forth,
The noblemen assembled soon after the sunrise,
Came forth with the king to listen to his counsel—
860 Unsullied knights all, who warred for Christ.

Vespasian gazes outward, looks on his men,
Who were fresher for fighting than when they began.[1]
He petitions the princes first—and all others after—
Each to say what he wishes concerning the war:

865 "For before this town and these high towers are taken,
Great hardship and trouble will be hard at hand."
They all turned to Titus and gave him the floor
To talk about the city and siege and to speak for them all.

Then Titus turns to them and begins to talk:
870 "To fight thus with the faithless will be worse for us,
For they are bold in their defense, fierce men and noble,
And this towered town is so tough to win.

The worst wretch in the place can lie in wait on the wall,
Can throw down one stone and stun many knights,
875 As we hesitate and stare and do little real harm,
And ever the worst wounds of war are inflicted on us!

They should not now be permitted to leave for more food:
If we cease combat until they consume their supplies,
We will hunt them with hunger and chase them from the city
880 Without suffering harm or wound or any more sorrow.[2]

---

1   *Who were fresher ... when they began*   Cf. line 609. The claim that the Roman soldiers
    were rested and refreshed is odder now, since they were severely wounded this time and
    stayed up all night dancing and listening to music. Time and exhaustion will affect the
    Jews inside the city more predictably.

2   *They should not ... any more sorrow*   Titus argues that they will not win the city by
    means of combat, so that warfare of any kind is useless. He proposes that they simply
    maintain position and permit no safe conducts (what we might now call humanitar-
    ian missions). Cut off from supplies and water, the inhabitants of Jerusalem will then
    slowly starve to death without harming the Romans, and those who do survive will
    give up the city in search for food.

For where food is scarce, there strength fails,
And where hunger is hot, there hearts are feeble."
Pleased, all assented to this speech that pertained to the siege,
Which was just what the prince and people desired.

Constables were called to the king then,   885
Marshals and macers,[1] men that he trusted.
He commanded them kindly, no matter what might happen,
To guard the walls with a watch of well-chosen men:

"For we wish to go deer hunting in the nearby heath
And listen to the dogs run along rugged shores,   890
Ride to the riverbank and flush out the birds,
See falcons fly, strike down the best—[2]

Each man may proceed to what pleasure he pleases!"
Princes come out from their tents, ride off on their steeds.
They take part in tournaments,[3] waste time, wait on the town.   895
This life they led for a long time. Our Lord grant us joy!

Passus 5

Nero has now caused much misery in Rome,
Tortured the Pope to death and killed many people—
St. Paul with St. Peter, the prince of apostles,
Seneca and the senators—and set fire to the city.   900

---

1   *Constables were called ... Marshals and macers*   Military officers of different ranks in
    this context, but these are also terms for members of a medieval noble retinue. A
    constable is a chief managerial officer, a *marshal* is a chief officer in a royal household,
    and a *macer* (mace-bearer) is also an official with ceremonial or legal administrative
    duties. In other words, Vespasian sounds like the lord of a fourteenth-century English
    household—a characterization that the final anachronistic quatrains of this passus cor-
    roborate.
2   *For we wish ... down the best*   Vespasian's sudden decision to go hunting is a decidedly
    weird turn of events, but hunting and hawking is conventional activity for popular me-
    dieval romance heroes. In terms of the poem's narrative progression, the point is that
    Vespasian responds to the ceasefire by permitting furloughs and associated recreations.
3   *tournaments*   Medieval combat exercises, jousting contests between mounted knights
    in armor.

He murdered his mother and his mild wife too,
And harmed many Christians who believed in Christ.[1]
When the Romans saw this cruelty, right away they rose up
To kill quickly the emperor who had so upset them.

905   Crowds pushed to the palace, the poor and all others,
To kill the impudent king in his magnificent fortress.
Both the senators and the citizens together agreed:
Nothing else could be done: they had decided his sentence.

Then that man flew, friendless and alone,
910   To a private outhouse—and the people pursued.
He took the branch of a tree: he carried nothing else,
Though he had on this earth so much glowing gold.

He tugged with his teeth and bit on that branch
'Til it was sharp at the point like the tip of a spike.
915   Then that man paused, and he spoke bitterly.
To all people there he said these words out loud:

"Get back, you traitors! No boor with his booze
Will ever tell tale of how he killed his own king!"
He stabs himself with that spike, straight into the heart
920   So the core of it cleft—and then the king died.[2]

This trouble occurred six months and no more
After Vespasian had gone to make war on the Jews:

---

1   *murdered his mother ... believed in Christ* These lines and the previous quatrain cover
not only the time since Titus and Vespasian left Rome but the events of several years:
Nero's mother Agrippina died in 59 CE, and her murder was a popular medieval image
of tyrannical cruelty; the Great Fire of Rome occurred in July 64 CE; Nero's pregnant
second wife Poppaea Sabina died in 65 CE, and it was generally believed that her hus-
band kicked her to death; Nero ordered Seneca, his teacher and advisor, to kill himself
in 65 CE; and Peter and Paul were martyred sometime between 64 and 66 CE, amidst
an early outbreak of Roman persecution of Christians. Cf. "In Context" section C.3.

2   *the king died* Nero died 9 June 68. The poet follows medieval Christian legendary ac-
counts of his death (see "In Context" section C.3 for an example). What follows is the
tumultuous "year of the four emperors," a series of short reigns that led to the accession
of Vespasian.

Four miles from Rome—it will always be remembered—
A man once emperor of all thus ended in misfortune.

Great men got together to decide on another: 925
First on Galba,[1] a man who had had many troubles
With Otho Lucius,[2] a lord who long hated him.
And at the last that man took his life from him:

In the marketplace in Rome, the two of them met.
Otho struck him down dead, gave grievous wounds   930
To the man who had ruled for just four months or more—
And then that duke[3] died, and left the diadem behind.

When Galba was gone and put in the ground,
In came Otho eagerly, and as emperor was crowned.
The man was in his majesty for only three months,   935
And he gave his soul to Satan and so slew himself.

The Romans promoted a man to protect Rome,
A knight named Vitellius,[4] and the crown passed to him.

...................................[5]

But for the sake of Sir Sabin, a man well renowned,
Vespasian's brother by blood, whom he had murdered...[6]   940

....

---

1 *Galba* Emperor from June 68–January 69 CE.
2 *Otho Lucius* Marcus Salvius Otho was emperor from January–April 69 CE, and his
   reign ended in suicide. The poet follows other medieval historians in mistakenly calling
   the emperor by his father's name (Lucius Otho).
3 *that duke* Galba.
4 *Vitellius* Emperor from September–December 69 CE.
5 ... At this point the text is badly corrupted. Lines concerning Vitellius' reign and
   conflict with Vespasian have certainly been lost, although it is unclear how many.
6 *Sir Sabin, a ... he had murdered* Not Sir Sabin of Syria, who is at Jerusalem, but Titus
   Flavius Sabinus, Vespasian's brother, whom Vitellius had killed in December 69 CE.

To avenge on Vitellius the death of his brother,
Vespasian sent men from Syria to Rome.

....

So that the new emperor, naked as a needle,
He[1] dragged through the city for Sir Sabin's sake.

945 Then they butchered the glutton like a disemboweled beast
So that all of his guts fell into his undergarments.
Down he went screaming and surrendered his soul,
And they took up his corpse and threw it in the Tiber.[2]

Seven months this man held the scepter in hand,
950 And he lost his life like this because of evil deeds.
Another man for the scepter was then to be sought—
For all these nobles are gone and will never return.

Now I will say more about the city and the siege,
How this worthy king[3] who wars for Christ
955 Has held in the heathens this second half winter,[4]
So that none have been so brave as to exit the city.

As he was sitting with his dukes at dinner one day,
Men arrived from Rome, rushing to him quickly
In bright mail-coats and armor, and with a new message.
960 All bowed down to the lord and gave him his letters.

They say: "Worthy king, the knighthood of Rome,
By assent of the senators and all the rest of the city,

---

1   *He*   Presumably one of Vespasian's men.
2   *Then they butchered ... in the Tiber*   Vitellius was killed by Vespasian's troops. The details here are legendary and reflect Vitellius' reputation for gluttony.
3   *this worthy king*   Vespasian.
4   *winter*   Year, as with "winters" at line 23; also an expression that contrasts with the "summer time" in which Caiaphas was killed (see line 708). The poem does not follow the historical length of the siege of Jerusalem, which lasted just over 140 days. Cf. line 1173.

Have chosen you commander, to be their chief lord
And strong emperor at Rome. So say these letters."[1]

The lord unfolds the leaf,[2] examines these letters,   965
Looks over each line from beginning to end.
The tables are cleared, and the man rises up,
Calls a council quickly and then makes this speech:

"You are men of my blood,[3] for whom I want the best.
My son is closest to me, and others are like family: 970
Sir Sabin of Syria, a man whom I trust,
And several good friends who owe me allegiance.

A happy message is now delivered from Rome
To make me lord of that land, as these letters report.
Sir Sabin of Syria, it is fitting that you say   975
How I might save myself and also do this,

For I have solemnly sworn to remain right here
Until I have bent to my will this whole towered town
And they give up the keys and the gates have been won
And this stronghold brought down on those who defend it—   980

To batter and break down these high barricades
So no stone in that place will ever stand on another.[4]
Give your counsel, sir knight," the king said to him,
"For I will act at your wisdom, if honor accords."

Then straightaway says Sir Sabin: "Illustrious lord,   985
We are warriors with you, to advance your honor,
Long committed to you, and we are your men.
What we do is your deed. No man may judge else."

---

1   *the knighthood ... say these letters* The Roman senate declared Vespasian emperor in
    December 69 CE.

2   *leaf* Page (of a letter).

3   *blood* Lineage or temperament, not a biological designation in this case.

4   *no stone in ... stand on another* Reaffirmation of the vow at lines 355–56 and an echo
    of the biblical prophecy in Matthew 24.2 and Luke 19.42–44, also invoked at lines
    1019–20 and 1289.

There adjudged was the judgment: he who acts through another
990 Shall still be the sovereign when the deed has been done.[1]
For the man who holds the foot down at the far end,
Is as fierce as the man who flays off the flesh.[2]

"Charge your son Titus to capture this town,
And his brother Domitian,[3] the daring bold duke.
995 I hereby hold up my hand: as long as my heart beats,
I will remain here with them, with all the army I have.

And you shall ride into Rome and receive the crown
To become emperor with honor, as your destiny dictates.
Thus may your covenant with Christ be maintained:
1000 You do yourself what your soldiers do by your order."

Then with a lion's look he[4] lifted his eyes,
Went quickly to Titus and told him the tale.
And he swiftly assents to what Sir Sabin has said,
With his brother and the soldiers, as if to salute him:[5]

1005 "I will stay at this town until I have taken it
And made roads through the walls for wagons and carts,
To keep both of our vows, if luck will allow it,
Or be chopped into pieces before I can leave."

A book on a broad shield was brought in for swearing:
1010 All barons kissed it and stretched forth their hands,

---

1   *adjudged was the ... has been done*   I.e., the decision of the council, written by the poet
    to sound like a legal formula, is that Vespasian will not abandon his vow to destroy
    Jerusalem, since he still gives the orders, even if other men carry them out. Restated
    more simply at line 1000.
2   *For the man ... off the flesh*   Deer-butchering metaphor: the person who holds the
    animal in place is as strong as the one who is skinning it. The proverb matches similar
    comparisons elsewhere in the poem. Cf. lines 879, 945, 1132, and 1308.
3   *Domitian*   Titus' younger brother, who was emperor 81–96 CE.
4   *he*   Vespasian.
5   *he swiftly assents ... to salute him*   I.e., Titus agrees to take over command of the siege
    and behaves deferentially toward Vespasian.

Pledged to be loyal to that lord who would lead them,
To Sir Titus, the true[1] king, until they could capture the city.

Then was that man[2] as delighted as a day-bird,
Kissed his knights quickly with these concerned words:
"My wealth and my honor you have power to protect,   1015
For upon this town hangs the treasure of my troth.[3]

This town cannot go untaken, nor these high towers,
Not for all the glowing gold found in God's kingdom,
Nor can any stone in the place be left standing aloft
But must be overturned and toppled, the Temple and all."   1020

Thus he takes his leave from all of his men,
Walks weeping away and gazes at the walls,
As he goes prays to God to send them His grace
To hold to their promise and never change heart.

Now Vespasian is gone over whales' streams[4]   1025
Has entered right into Rome and been made emperor,
And Titus has had so much joy at these tidings
That a sickness in his sinews suddenly afflicts him.[5]

The man, for delight at his dear father's bliss,
Was seized so severely with cramps and with cold   1030
That the fingers and feet, the fists and the joints,
Were limp as a leek and had lost all their strength,

---

1   *true*   Rightful, emphasizing the official transfer of power that is completed as the men
    perform homage to their new commander. Cf. lines 1–2.
2   *that man*   Vespasian.
3   *treasure of my troth*   Most important part of my (legal) obligation.
4   *whales' streams*   Sea.
5   *And Titus has ... suddenly afflicts him*   I.e., Titus is so happy he gets sick. Not original
    to the poet, this episode comes from legendary sources. See "In Context" section C.2.

Grew very crippled and unnaturally crooked,
And many men wept when they saw him this way.
1035 They sent word to the city and sought a physician
Who could cure the king and confer a safe conduct.[1]

When they searched with their men throughout the whole city,
They could not find a man to accomplish the feat,
Save Josephus—the same—who was an excellent surgeon,
1040 And he consented to attempt a cure for the man.

When he had come to the king and discovered the cause,
And how this man had fallen into sickness so quickly,
Until he could complete his cure he requested safe conduct
For whatever man he might want to bring from the city.[2]

1045 The king was glad to grant anything the man wanted—
And he[3] walks away from him then and swiftly returns
With a man that the proud king very keenly despised,
And brings the attendant right up to his bedside.

When suddenly Titus turned eyes on that man,
1050 Hot anger rose so violently into his heart
That the blood began to move all about in the veins
And the sinews returned to their natural form.[4]

The feet and all features are just as before,
Have regained their right nature, and so the king rises,

---

1   *safe conduct*   Guarantee of ceasefire or personal protection that allows a person to
     travel without fear of harm. The Romans seek a doctor from Jerusalem but also need
     someone with the authority to grant them safe passage in and out of the city.
2   *Until he could ... from the city*   I.e., because Josephus has been brought out of the city
     to treat Titus, he now also requires safe conduct to go back to the city and return with
     another man.
3   *he*   Josephus, who now fetches an anonymous Jewish combatant whom Titus evi-
     dently knows and hates.
4   *When suddenly Titus ... their natural form*   Josephus resolves an imbalance of humors,
     the four chief bodily fluids that, in medieval medical theories, determine physical and
     mental health. Titus' joy caused too much phlegm, or cold (line 1030), and Josephus
     manipulates Titus' anger to produce a hot, or choleric, response.

Thanks God for his grace and the good physician   1055
For all—except for bringing his enemy to him.

Then says Josephus: "This man here has helped you,
And he has been your cure, though you want to harm him.
Therefore grant him your grace in return for his good,
And be friend to your foe, who is worthy of friendship."   1060

The king reconciled with the man who had saved him,
And there granted him grace to go where he wished.
He rejoiced with Josephus and offered him jewels:
Brooches and bezants, rings and bracelets of gold.

But the man[1] forsakes all and goes back to the city   1065
With safe conduct, as he came—he keeps nothing more.
And Titus besieges the town, where trouble is on hand,
Because a hard and hot hunger is now come upon them.

It is difficult to tell about the trouble in the town,
What death and disaster has occurred because of food: 1070
For forty days before this they had nothing to eat,
Neither fish nor flesh[2] for a man to bite down on.

Neither was there bread, soup, nor broth, nor a beast alive,[3]
Neither wine to drink nor water, except what they wept.[4]
Old shields and shoes they were eagerly eating—   1075
That fare was dreadful for the womenfolk to chew.

They fell down because of the lack, flat on the ground,
Dead as door nails, many hundred each day.
Sorrow stirred up thick: they behaved like wolves:
Strong men filled their bellies through war on the weak.   1080

---

1   *the man*   Josephus.
2   *flesh*   Meat.
3   *a beast alive*   An animal that could be butchered for meat, as opposed to the dead flesh
      (i.e., leather) of the shields and shoes in the following lines.
4   *Neither wine to drink ... they wept*   I.e., they drank their own tears.

One Mary, a mild woman, because of absence of food,
Cooked on the coals her own baby, whom she bore.[1]
She roasts the spine and the ribs, with pitiful words,
Says: "Son, upon each side is our sorrow increased:

1085 Battle is outside the city to slaughter our bodies,
Hunger is so hot within that our hearts nearly burst.
Therefore give up what I gave you, and turn back again,
Enter where you came out"—and she eats a shoulder.

Then the smell of the roast rose into the street,
1090 So that many starving people smelled the aroma.
They bashed down the door: the woman must die
Who in this misfortune concealed meat from men.

Then the worthy woman says, in a wild hunger:
"I have cooked my own baby and gnawed on the bones,
1095 But I have saved some for you." And she fetches a side
Of the baby, whom she bore—and all their blood[2] changes.

They walked away weeping bitterly for woe,
And saying: "Alas! How long shall we dwell in this life?[3]
It is better yet to die in an instant in battle
1100 Than to live on thus in misery and lengthen our end."

They adjudged then a judgment that was anguish to hear:
To remove through vile death all who used up provisions—

---

1   *One Mary, a ... whom she bore*   Versions of this episode commonly occur in the Ven-
    geance of Our Lord tradition (cf. "In Context" section C.2). Allusion to the Virgin
    Mary is likely deliberate, so that the scene becomes a literalized Eucharistic image.
    Medieval Christian fantasies that Jews killed children, or stories of familial sacrifice
    during sieges, may also be relevant. For more information and related texts, see the
    Introduction above, as well as "In Context" sections A.3 (which includes the Middle
    English text for comparison) and D.1-4.
2   *their blood*   The complexions, or moods, of those who have beaten down her door.
3   *Alas! How long ... in this life*   Cf. Psalm 13.1-2, Psalm 79.5, and Revelation 6.10.

Women, and the weak people who were of old age
Or could not stand in place but depleted their stores—[1]

And to offer truce afterwards, discuss terms with the lord.[2]   1105
But Titus grants nothing, because of guile they intend,
For he is wise who is wary of woe in advance,
And it is best to deal with deceit from a distance.

They plotted to make pathways under the walls,
When Titus refused to grant the town truce.   1110
With miners and masons they started to mine.
Fast they are digging into the ground—and God give us joy!

Passus 6

After some time, as Titus rides around the city
With just sixty spearmen pulled from the siege,
Far away from full flanks—then out of a cave   1115
An ambush of shimmering helmets[3] attacked:

Five hundred fighting men fell about them,
In jupons and greaves.[4] They were Jews.
They had made a pathway and mined under the wall—
And Titus turns toward them without another word.   1120

Lances were soon broken, shields were shredded,
And many men spear-gored with a sharp end.
Beaming iron and mail-coats were all drenched in blood,
And many men at that assault sought the ground.[5]

---

1   *To remove through ... depleted their stores*   I.e., the Jews decide to kill all those who use
   up supplies but cannot fight or otherwise contribute to the city's defense.
2   *the lord*   Titus.
3   *shimmering helmets*   Men in armor.
4   *jupons and greaves*   Armor-covering tunics (sometimes with coats of arms) and leg
   armors.
5   *And many men ... sought the ground*   I.e., many involved in that battle hit the ground
   (fell and died).

1125 They hack upon hard steel with a will so savage
That spark-fires fly forth as if from flint-stones:
The heads and the helmets are hewn off together,
The stumps[1] remain in their steel, under horse hooves.

The young duke Domitian heard of this noise
1130 And sallied forth from the army with eight hundred spearmen
Who fall on the false men and round them up quickly.
He butchers them all like beasts, and so helps his brother.

Then Titus turns quickly back toward his tents,
Commands miners and others to go stop the mining.[2]
1135 He proffers peace after this, because he felt pity
When he realized the sorrow of those who were trapped.

But the crafty man John, who was in charge of the Jews,
And another, Simon,[3] in assent with him, forsook the offer.
They said they would rather remain in life as they were
1140 Than have any man from Rome rejoice in their sorrow.

All commerce in the city had ceased by then:
There was nothing to buy with bezants that a man could eat.
For a farthing's worth of food, florins[4] were offered—
Princes in the city would push a hundred into hands.

1145 But all was incurable agony—for whoever had bread
Would not have given a crumb for all the wealth in the world.
Women quickly grew pale and their faces changed:
Maidens once so fair are now feeble and fall down,

---

1   *stumps*   The stumps of the heads, i.e., the bodies.
2   *Commands miners … stop the mining*   I.e., Titus sends his own miners to stop the
    Jewish miners from tunneling under the walls.
3   *the crafty man … another, Simon*   John of Gischala and Simon bar Giora, Jewish rebels
    who became powerful discordant forces during the siege. Most historical accounts cite
    their disdain for each other and penchant for tyranny and exploitation of the weak.
    The poet emphasizes Jewish unity here, but cf. lines 1079–80.
4   *For a farthing's … florins*   A farthing is a quarter of a penny (a very small amount), a
    florin a gold coin worth a great deal more.

Swoon, swell like swine, and some turn black.
Some are as lean as lantern-horns[1] to behold.   1150
The mortality was so enormous that no man could say
Where in the town the dead bodies could be buried,

So they carried them to the wall and threw them all over—
Into the deep of the ditches the dead fall down.
When Titus was told the tale, he swore to the true God   1155
That he had offered them peace and had great pity.

He begged Josephus to preach, to instruct the people
To save themselves then and surrender the city.
But John forsook the entreaty to act in this way,
He and Simon, that other who had charge of the city.   1160

Many people leave the town because of the preaching
Come out at the side gates, and then Titus seeks
To absolve them of the wrong they did unto God,
And he grants them grace and commits them to jailors.

But when they found meat, their strength was so faint,   1165
They lacked any power to digest any food:
Each one had guts stuffed full of gold:
Lest their foes steal them, they had eaten their florins!

When the trick was discovered and brought to clear sight,
The men slaughtered them all without leave of their lord: 1170
They gore every man open and take out the gold,
More eager for florins than for the men's lives.

And the gates remained untaken until two years had gone—[2]
This long they sought the city by siege before they had it.
Eleven hundred thousand Jews in that time   1175
Died by sword and by hunger, while the war lasted.

---

1 *lantern-horns* Thin panes of glass that protect and distribute lantern light.
2 *two years had gone* Historically, the siege was much shorter than this. Cf. line 955,
   where a similar timeline is suggested.

Now Titus has taken counsel to attack the town,
To win it from werewolves' hands[1] by any means,
Never to offer them pity nor peace any more,
1180 Nor allow any grace to any man captured.

They all equip themselves quickly for battle,
Go right to the town with trumpets and pipes,
With great din and drummers draw near the walls,
Where many mighty and strong men stand above.

1185 Sir Sabin of Syria went to one side.
The young duke Domitian went to another.
Fifteen thousand fighting men each man had,
With many kinds of engines, and miners enough.

Titus, at the town gate with ten thousand helmets,
1190 Shows the miners where they should mine at the wall,
Sets up siege engines for an assault on both sides,
And puts brave mail-clad men into tall towers.

There was nothing but outcry and clamor, as if all would die,
Each living life lain down on another.
1195 At each battlement were screams and clashing of weapons,
And many men in one moment were beaten to death.

Sir Sabin of Syria, as the combat continues,
Leans a ladder and climbs hard up the wall,
Wins his way onto it—though woe came to him—
1200 And despite stones and steel-works[2] stands up tall.

He slew six on the wall, Sir Sabin alone—
But the seventh strikes him a brutal blow,
So that the brain bursts out at both nostrils,
And Sabin falls into the ditch, dead from the blow.

---

1   *werewolves' hands*   The hands of the Jews, abusively construed as half-beast monsters.
    One of the earliest uses of the word in the English language. Cf. line 1079.
2   *stones and steel-works*   Projectiles thrown at Sabin by Jewish forces.

Then for some time Titus curses and cries,   1205
For he has lost the man he was always to love:
"For now a duke is dead, I think the most daring
Who ever mounted a steed or donned any steel."

Then Titus sets up a siege engine on the same side,
An engine built for the battle, and drives it into the wall,   1210
So that all men where it hits are thrown over.
A hundred die at that blow and fall into the ditch.

Then Titus throws up a hand and thanks the Heaven-King
That they[1] have so dearly paid for the death of the duke.
The Jews beg for peace—this was right at Passover—[2]   1215
And they hand over the gate keys to the worthy king.

"No, traitors," said Titus. "Take them for yourselves,
For no guard from your wall will now show us the way:
We have won the gates for ourselves, against your will—
That will bitterly be turned upon your accursed race!"   1220

Before the gates were won, throughout the whole year,[3]
Miraculous things were seen all over the city.
A bright burning sword hung over the town
Without help or hand except Heaven's alone.

Armed men in the air appeared like an army   1225
And were seen over the city on several occasions.
Against nature, a calf delivered in the Temple
And gave birth to a girl lamb at the offering time.[4]

---

1   *they*   The Jews.
2   *this was right at Passover*   This does not follow the historical timeline—the destruction
    of the city and the Temple occurred in late September 70 CE—but it does link the con-
    clusion of the siege to the initial Roman assault, and to the time of Christ's crucifixion.
    Cf. lines 161 and 320.
3   *throughout the whole year*   All portents listed come from the poet's historical sources,
    though the timeline is compressed.
4   *Against nature ... the offering time*   Reference to the ritual sacrifice of the red heifer in
    Numbers 19.1–10, a type of offering made in the Temple. Accounts of this event were
    interpreted by Christians as symbolic of the new Christian law superseding the old
    Jewish law (including offerings in the Temple), which the sacrifice of Christ (the lamb
    of God) had made irrelevant. For the theological argument, see Hebrews 9.13–14.

A man on the wall cried wondrously loudly:
1230 "Voice from the east, voice from the west, voice from the four
    winds!"
He said, "Woe, woe, woe shall befall you,
Jerusalem the Jews' town and the fair Temple!"[1]

Just as the city was conquered and won,
The man on the wall said yet one more saying:
1235 "Woe to this noble place, and woe to myself!"
And he died when he had finished, from a blow from a sling.

And then the wicked reflected and considered them vengeance,[2]
And they blamed their great sorrow on the wrong they had done
When they slew in the city the bishop St. James—[3]
1240 None equated with Christ the misfortune they had.

Still their gates opened up, and they surrendered themselves
Without mail-coats or bright garb but in their bare shirts.
From noon until dark night, there was never an end,
But ever man after man was pleading for mercy.

1245 Titus makes his way into the town:
No one could stay in the street for the stench of dead bodies.
People strewn in pathways were a pity to see.
They were starved and disfigured when the food disappeared.

There was nothing but lean bones left on the ladies,
1250 Who before this were fleshy and fair to behold.
Citizens with bellies like barrels before then,
Now no bigger than a greyhound to grip at the waist.

---

1 *Woe, woe ... the fair Temple* Cf. Revelation 8.13, Jeremiah 13.27, and Isaiah 62.6.
2 *then the wicked ... considered them vengeance* I.e., the Jews considered the miraculous
   portents a sign of vengeance.
3 *the bishop St. James* St. James the Less, called the "brother of the Lord" in Galatians
   1.19 and traditionally considered the first bishop of Jerusalem (based on Acts 15 and
   21.17–18). The poet's historical and legendary sources describe his martyrdom at the
   Temple, somewhere between 57 and 62 CE, as the result of an attack by an angry Jewish
   mob. Cf. "In Context" section C.2.

Titus does not tarry for that but turns to the Temple,
Which on the roof was adorned with enormous rubies.
With pearls and peridots,[1] the whole place appeared   1255
As a glowing coal-fire that flickers against gold.

The doors were studded thick full of diamonds
And made a marvelous flame with glistening pearls,
So they shone like a lamp, always shimmering light:
No candle needed kindling when clerks would arise.   1260

The Romans gape at the work, cursing the time
That ever so precious a place should perish for sin.
Titus commands them to take out the treasures:
"Beat down the building. Burn it to the ground."

There were plenty of precious stones in the place: 1265
Great bars of gold for whoever wished to grab them,
Coins of great value, plates and polished vessels,
Basins of burnished gold and other bright gear,

Strongly built columns, made from many metals,
Skillfully cast in copper and in unsullied silver.   1270
Every part of the place was adorned with pure gold.
The Romans tore it all down and took it to Rome.[2]

When they had searched the city in a similar way,[3]
No tongue could tell of the treasures they found:
Jewels for fine men and valuable clasps—   1275
No one lacked florins of fine gold there!—

Rich fur and fabric for princes to wear,
Bezants, gold bracelets, brooches, and rings,

---

1   *peridots*   Green gemstones.
2   *The Romans tore ... it to Rome*   An image of the Roman looting can still be seen on
    the triumphal Arch of Titus in Rome, which shows Titus' men carrying items from the
    Temple, notably the large menorah. See this volume's cover image for a detail.
3   *a similar way*   The same way they searched the Temple, i.e., through inventory and
    plunder.

Many cartfuls of clothes made of clean silk.
1280 No one lacked wealth but chose what he liked!

Now the masons and miners have probed the soil,
Have pierced the walls with pickaxes and punches:
They hack through hard stones, hurl them to earth,
So the ditches are darkened with dust from the powder.

1285 Thus they worked at the wall a full week's time,
Until the city was surveyed and thoroughly searched.
All at once they laid waste to where the wall stood,
Both the Temple and its tower—all the town over.[1]

No stone in that place was standing aloft—[2]
1290 Made with mortar or mud, all walls fell to dust.
Neither timber nor tree, Temple nor else,
Was not beaten to the ground and burned to black earth.

And when the Temple was razed, Titus commanded
Hands to the plows to plow the whole place.[3]
1295 They sowed it with salt and then said these words:
"Now is this fortified place forever destroyed."

Afterwards Titus set himself upon a rich seat,
As a justice himself to judge all the Jews.
Criers called them forth as those who killed Christ
1300 And asked Pilate to appear, who was provost then.

Pilate comes out, appears in the court,
And with courteous words he inquires of the man[4]
About the scorn that Christ suffered, and the hard wounds,
When He ended His days and went to His death.

---

1   *All at once ... the town over*   The Western Wall in Jerusalem is the remnant of the outer
    wall of the destroyed Temple complex.
2   *No stone in ... was standing aloft*   Fulfillment of gospel prophecy (Matthew 24.2 and
    Luke 19.42–44), and an honoring of Titus' and Vespasian's vows. Cf. lines 355–56,
    982, and 1019–20.
3   *Hands to the ... the whole place*   Cf. Jeremiah 26.18.
4   *he inquires of the man*   Titus inquires of Pilate.

Then the man spoke and recounted the story, 1305
How the whole deed was done when He endured death:
His apostle[1] sold Him for thirty pennies in a pouch.
Thus was he bargained for and bought and killed like a beast.

"Now is he damned," said the king, "who made that deal.
He collected that money and turned merchant in error, 1310
To sell so precious a prince for so few pennies,
Even if each farthing had been worth a hundred florins.

But before I leave here—this will be scorn to them—
I will make a deal, in memory of that one,
With all who wish to buy or bargain for their bodies 1315
At a price less than what they were paid for the prophet."[2]

He had a market announced in the midst of the army:
All who wished to purchase cheap would have purchases—
For the price of a penny, to whomever would pay,
Thirty Jews in a bundle, bundled with ropes.[3] 1320

Thus they were bargained for and bought and deprived of their
    land.
Never after would any of them enter that site,
Nor any dwell in that land who believed in their law,
Which tortured the true God. Thus Titus commands.

The noble[4] clerk Josephus was ordered to Rome, 1325
Where he made fair books about this matter and more.

---

1   *His apostle*   Judas Iscariot. John 12.6 and 13.29 provide the detail that Judas carried a
    bag.
2   *the prophet*   Jesus. Cf. line 15.
3   *He had a ... bundled with ropes*   This dramatic inversion of the sale of Jesus is not
    original to the poem. The specific transaction (thirty for a penny) is part of the Ven-
    geance of Our Lord tradition, but the selling of Jews after the destruction of Jerusalem
    is also recorded in the poet's historical sources. Cf. "In Context" section C.2.
4   *noble*   The equivalent Middle English word (*gentile*) usually means "noble" (related
    to Modern English "genteel" or "gentle," as in "gentleman"), but can occasionally
    mean "pagan" (i.e., simply non-Christian). A relationship between the two meanings
    is evident in Modern English "Gentile," which commonly means "non-Jewish" but
    biblically denotes nations other than God's chosen nation.

And Pilate was sent to prison to feel pain forever,
At Vienne,[1] where he suffered vile death and vengeance.

The man who watched him at one point
1330 Was eating some fruit and proffered a pear.
Eager to peel his pear, he pleaded for a knife—
And so the watchman tossed him the tool.

And with it he stuck himself to the heart,
And so died cursedly, as accursed as his line.[2]
1335 ....
....[3]

When all was finished and judged, they folded up tents,
Sounded the end of the siege and carried off treasure,
Went singing away, their pleasures promoted—
1340 And they are riding home to Rome. Now may our Lord guide
us!

Hic terminatur bellum Iudaicum apud Ierusalem.[4]

---

1 *Vienne* In the Rhone Valley region of France. It is historically extremely unlikely that
   Pilate was still in Jerusalem to begin with, but the poet is combining accounts from
   legendary and historical sources. Cf. "In Context" section C.1.
2 *his line* His ancestry, family.
3 .... The text is corrupted here. Editors hypothesize that two lines are lost.
4 *Hic terminatur bellum Iudaicum apud Ierusalem* Latin: Here ends the war against the
   Jews at Jerusalem.

In Context

A. The Middle English *Siege of Jerusalem*

The Siege of Jerusalem was written in Middle English alliterative verse between 1370 and 1390 CE, in the northwest Midlands of England. Though evidence for date and provenance of anonymous medieval works is often difficult to interpret, dialect features and histories of surviving manuscript copies of the poem suggest that it was probably written by someone who lived in the border region of Lancashire and West Yorkshire, and that its author may have been a canon at Bolton, an Augustinian priory in the Craven district of Yorkshire.[1] Six relatively complete copies of the poem are extant, and another three survive in fragments (including a single leaf that was used in the binding of another, later book). All of these are distinct handwritten copies from lost exemplars, all made within 100 years of the poem's composition. They were made by scribes and in dialects that cover many regions of England. From them we can hypothesize that many other copies once existed.[2]

One of the more challenging things to represent in a Modern English translation of *The Siege of Jerusalem* is its prosody. English poetry since Chaucer has been mainly based on the accentual syllabic line, but this poem is a particularly fine and accomplished example of late-medieval alliterative verse, a descendant of Anglo-Saxon (Old English) poetic style. It is written in the "alliterative long lines" that seem to have held a particular appeal for fourteenth-century English

---

1 See Hanna and Lawton, *The Siege*, xxx–xxxi and lii–liv; and Elisa Narin van Court, "*The Siege of Jerusalem* and Augustinian Historians: Writing About Jews in Fourteenth-Century England," *Chaucer Review* 29 (1995): 227–48. An argument against this localization has been posited by Ad Putter, Judith Jefferson, and Myra Stokes, *Studies in the Metre of Alliterative Verse* (Oxford: Society for the Study of Medieval Languages and Literature, 2007), 11–12.

2 For detailed information on the manuscripts, their dates, geographical associations, and contents, see Hanna and Lawton xiii–xxvii.

poets. (Notable Middle English alliterative works include *Piers Plowman*, *Sir Gawain and the Green Knight*, *Wynnere and Wastoure*, and *St Erkenwald*, as well as the historical romances *Morte Arthure*, *The Destruction of Troy*, and *The Wars of Alexander*, all of which contain passages that echo *The Siege of Jerusalem*.[1]) The rhythm of alliterative poetry is sound-based; it relies not on rhyme or syllables but on careful patterns of stressed alliterating sounds, which in turn are related to the syntax of each line. Rhythm and alliterative sound work together with grammar, syntax, and meaning to accomplish heightened rhetorical effect. Repetition of words and formulaic or appositive phrases add to this effect.

The alliterative meter of the Middle English *Siege of Jerusalem* is disciplined and regular (though there is variation). Each of its lines can be divided into two half lines, an a-verse and b-verse, separated by a caesura or pause in the middle, with the pattern aa(a)/ax. In this pattern, *a* represents the alliterating sound, which coincides with a stressed syllable, and *x* represents a stressed syllable that does not alliterate with *a*. There are usually two or three alliterating sounds in the a-verse, and usually only one in the b-verse. As is common for late-medieval alliterative poetry (this is part of what defines the "long line"), the number of intervening stressed or unstressed syllables varies. Take, for example, the opening eight lines of the poem:

>   a   a   /   a   x
> In **T**yberyus **t**yme, þe **t**rewe emperour,

>   a a   a / a   x
> **S**ire **S**esar hym**s**ulf **s**eysed in Rome

>   a   a   /   a   x
> Whyle **P**ylat was **p**rouost vndere þat **p**rince riche

>   a   a   /   a   x
> And **I**ewen **i**ustice also in **I**udees londe,

---

1   On alliterative genres and echoes of *Siege* in these works, see Livingston 10–15; Hanna and Lawton xxxv–xxxviii; and the Introduction above.

	a	(a)		a	/	a		x

a   (a)   a   /   a   x

Herode vndere his emperie— as heritage wolde   5

a   a   /   a   x

Kyng of Galile ycalled—,   whan þat Crist deyed

    a   a   /   a   x

Þey Sesar sakles were   þat oft synne hatide,

     a   a   /   a   x

Þrow Pylat pyned he was   and put on þe rode.

While the alliterating sound is normally an initial consonant (like the "t" in line 1), the stressed sound may also occur mid-word (as with "hymsulf" in line 2), and the pattern can also be organized around a vowel sound, that is, through assonance. For instance, line 5 is organized around the "e" sound rather than the initial "h," which may or may not be vocalized depending on dialect, and the "u/v" sound in "vndere" may be part of the pattern in this instance.

In the facsimile of an opening page of the poem provided here on page 93—from Oxford, Bodleian Library, MS Laud Misc. 656, the manuscript considered to be the best early and most complete example of the poem, used as the basis of all editions of the Middle English currently published—one can see that the basic alliterative units are maintained by the scribe. That is, the scribe maintains poetic line divisions and consistently marks the mid-line caesura with punctuation (he uses what looks like an inverted semicolon, called a *punctus elevatus*). He does not, however, use other punctuation or capitalization, nor mark quatrain or stanza divisions, all of which modern editors provide. The visual organization of the page is dependent on the alliterative line itself, more than anything else, so much so that the scribe (as all other scribes who copied the poem) does not notice the two lines that are lost after line 26. This corruption, a product of the transmission of the text over time, is observed only by editors who have reconstructed the quatrain units underlying the poem's structure and therefore have felt confident in hypothesizing a loss at this point in the text.

Three brief Middle English excerpts of the poem are printed below, alongside their corresponding Modern English translation. These passages provide a small sample of the poem's original appearance and language. They also show a glimpse of the editing and translation process, and allow some close reading based on the Middle English vocabulary and prosody. The first excerpt matches the opening page of the Laud manuscript, shown here. The two passages that follow reflect some of the poem's dramatic preoccupations: the episode in which Caiaphas and his clerks are captured, one of many effective battle scenes (favorites of alliterative poets); and the episode in which the starving Jewish Mary eats her own child, one of several emotionally arresting scenes of Jewish suffering in the poem.

The opening lines of *The Siege of Jerusalem* in Oxford, Bodleian Library MS Laud Misc. 656, folio 1v (late fourteenth century). Reproduced by permission of the Bodleian Library, University of Oxford.

1. Prologue, lines 1–35
(the Crucifixion, introduction of Titus and Vespasian)

In Tyberyus tyme,   þe trewe emperour,
Sire Sesar hymsulf   seysed in Rome
Whyle Pylat was prouost   vndere þat prince riche
And Iewen iustice also   in Iudees londe,

5 Herode vndere his emperie—   as heritage wolde
   Kyng of Galile ycalled—,   whan þat Crist deyed
   Þey Sesar sakles were   þat oft synne hatide,
   Þrow Pylat pyned he was   and put on þe rode.

   A pyler pyȝt was doun   vpon þe playn erþe,
10 His body bonden þerto   and beten with scourgis:
   Whyppes of quyrboyle   vmbywente his white sides
   Til al on rede blode ran   as rayn in þe strete.

   Suþ stoked on a stole   with styf mannes hondis,
   Blyndfelled as a be   and boffetis hym raȝte;
15 "Ȝif þou be prophete of pris,   prophecie," þey sayde,
   "Whiche berne hereaboute   bobbed þe laste?"

   A þrange þornen croune   þraste on his hed,
   Vmbecasten with a cry   and on croys slowen.
   For al þe harme þat he hadde   hasted he noȝt
20 On hem þe vyleny to venge   þat his veynys brosten,

   Bot ay taried on þe tyme   ȝif þey tourne wolde;
   Ȝaf hem space þat hym spilide,   þey hit spedde lyte,
   xl. wynter as Y fynde   and no fewere ȝyrys
   Or princes presed in hem   þat hym to pyne wroȝt.

25 Til hit tydde on a tyme   on Tytus of Rome
   Þat alle Gascoyne gate   and Gyan þe noble
   ...
   ...

In the time of Tiberius, Sir Caesar true,
The rightful emperor who ruled in Rome,
When Pilate was provost under that rich prince
And also judge of Jews in Judean lands,

Herod, under his rule, and by hereditary right,   5
Was called king of Galilee, when Christ died.
Though Caesar was spotless (he hated sin),
Through Pilate He was pained and put on the rood.

A pillar was placed plain on the ground,
His body bound to it and beaten with scourges.   10
Whips of loose leather hit His white sides
Until He ran red with blood, as rain runs in the street.

Then strong men's hands set Him on a stool,
Blindfolded Him like a bee and beat Him raw.
"If you are a prophet of price, prophesy!" they said.   15
"Which man among us walloped you last?"

A tight thorn crown was thrust on His head.
They crowded Him with a cry and killed Him on a cross.
For all the harm He had, He was not in a hurry
To avenge the villainy of those who burst His veins.   20

But He waited a while, in case they would convert,
Gave the guilty space, though it did little good—
Forty winters, as I find, and no fewer years—
Before princes pounced on those who wrought His pain,

Until the time came that Titus of Rome,   25
Who ruled all of Gascony and guarded Guyenne
…
…

Whyle noye neȝet hym   to in Neroes tyme.
30 He hadde a malady vnmeke   inmyddis þe face;
Þe lyppe lyþ on a lumpe   lyuered on þe cheke.
So a canker vnclene   hit cloched togedres.

Also his fadere of flesche   a ferly bytide:
A bikere of waspen bees   bredde in his nose,
35 Hyued vp in his hed—   he hadde hem of ȝouþe—

2. Passus 3, lines 573–608
(battle between Jews and Romans, Caiaphas and clerks captured)

Castels clateren doun,   cameles brosten,
Dromedaries to þe deþ   drowen ful swyþe;
575 Þe blode fomed hem fro   in flasches aboute
Þat kne-depe in þe dale   dascheden stedes.

Þe burnes in þe bretages   þat aboue were
For þe doust and þe dyn,   as alle doun ȝede
Whan hurdizs and hard erþe   hurtled togedre,
580 Al forstoppette in stele   starke-blynde wexen

And vnder dromedaries   diȝeden sone.
Was non left vpon lyue   þat alofte standeþ
Saue an anlepy olyfaunt   at þe grete ȝate
Þer as Cayphas þe clerke   in a castel rideþ.

585 He say þe wrake on hem wende   and away tourneþ
With twelf maystres ma   of Moyses lawe;
And hundred helmed men   hien hem after
Er þey of castel myȝt come,   cauȝten hem alle.

Bounden þe bischup   on a bycchyd wyse
590 Þat þe blode out barst   ilka band vndere,
And broȝten to þe berfray   alle þe bew-clerkes
Þer þe standard stode   and stadded hem þer.

A tribulation troubled him then, in Nero's time.
He had a severe sickness at the center of his face: 30
The lips lay in a clump, clotted on the cheek
Like an unclean tumor, clutched together.

A further wonder befell his fleshly father:
A nuisance of wasp-bees bred in his nose.
They hived in his head. He had had them since youth.   35

Castles clatter to the ground, camels burst open,
Dromedaries meet with their death very quickly—
The blood foamed from them into great motionless pools,   575
So that steeds were knee-deep as they dashed through the valley.

The men who were in the wooden structures on top,
As those defenses and the hard earth hurtled together,
Became utterly blind from the dust and the noise,
Were all smothered in steel, completely cut off,   580

And beneath fallen dromedaries they died on the spot.
There was none left alive even able to stand,
Save one single elephant there at the great gate,
Where Caiaphas the clerk rides in his castle.

He sees the destruction wrought and retreats   585
With twelve other masters of Moses' law.
A hundred helmeted men chase them in haste—
And they captured them before they could exit the castle.

They bound the bishop in so vile a way
That blood burst out from under each binding,   590
And they brought all the beaux-clerks up to the belfry,
Where the battle standard stood, and positioned them there.

Þe beste and þe britage   and alle þe briȝt gere,
Chaire and chaundelers   and charbokel stones,
595 Þe rolles þat þey redde on   and alle þe riche bokes
Þey broȝte myd þe bischup,   þou hym bale þouȝte.

Anon þe feyþles folke   fayleden herte,
Tourned toward þe toun   and Tytus hem after:
Felde of þe fals ferde,   in þe felde lefte,
600 An hundred in here helmes   myd his honde one.

Þe fals Iewes in þe felde   fallen so þicke
As hail froward heuen,   hepe ouer oþer.
So was þe bent ouerbrad,   blody byrunne,
With ded bodies aboute—   alle þe brod vale—

605 Myȝt no stede doun stap   bot on stele wede
Or on burne oþer on beste   or on briȝt scheldes.
So myche was þe multitude   þat on þe molde lafte
Þer so many were mart,   mereuail were ellis.

3. Passus 5, lines 1069–1100
(suffering in Jerusalem, Mary eats her child)

Now of þe tene in þe toun   were tore forto telle,
1070 What moryne and meschef   for mete is byfalle.
For fourty dayes byfor   þey no fode hadde,
Noþer fisch ne flesch   freke on to byte—

Bred, browet ne broþe,   ne beste vpon lyue,
Wyn ne water to drynke   bot wope of hemself.
1075 Olde scheldes and schone   scharply þey eten:
Þat liflode for ladies   was luþer to chewe.

Fellen doun for defaute,   flatte to þe grounde,
Ded as a dore-nayl,   eche day many hundred.
Wo wakned þycke: as wolues þey ferde—
1080 Þe wyght waried on þe woke   alle his wombe-fille.

With the bishop they brought (though it tormented him)
The beast and the castle and all the bright gear,
The chair and the candleholders and the carbuncle stones,   595
The scrolls that they read from and all precious books.

It was then that the faithless people lost heart.
They turned back to the town, with Titus pursuing.
He left many from the false army lying in the field:
A hundred in their helmets downed by his hand alone.   600

The false Jews in the field are fallen as thick
As hail from heaven, in heaps upon heaps.
So covered was the field, all the broad valley,
With the bodies of the dead, drenched in blood,

That no steed could step unless on steel clothes,   605
Or on a man, or on a beast, or on shining shields.
So great was the multitude that remained on the earth
Where so many were wounded—and a wonder if not!

It is difficult to tell about the trouble in the town,
What death and disaster has occurred because of food: 1070
For forty days before this they had nothing to eat,
Neither fish nor flesh for a man to bite down on.

Neither was there bread, soup, nor broth, nor a beast alive,
Neither wine to drink nor water, except what they wept.
Old shields and shoes they were eagerly eating—   1075
That fare was dreadful for the womenfolk to chew.

They fell down because of the lack, flat on the ground,
Dead as door nails, many hundred each day.
Sorrow stirred up thick: they behaved like wolves:
Strong men filled their bellies through war on the weak.   1080

On Marie, a myld wyf,   for meschef of foode,
Hire owen barn þat ȝo bare   brad on þe gledis,
Rostyþ rigge and rib   with rewful wordes,
Sayþ, "sone, vpon eche side   our sorow is alofte:

1085 Batail aboute þe borwe   our bodies to quelle;
Withyn hunger so hote   þat neȝ our herte brestyþ.
Þerfor ȝeld þat I þe ȝaf   and aȝen tourne,
Entre þer þou out cam,"   and etyþ a schouldere.

Þe rich roos of þe rost   riȝt in to þe strete
1090 Þat fele fastyng folke   felden þe sauere.
Doun þei daschen þe dore,   dey scholde þe berde
Þat mete yn þis meschef   hadde from men layned.

Þan saiþ þat worþi wif   in a wode hunger,
"Myn owen barn haue I brad   and þe bones gnawen,
1095 Ȝit haue I saued ȝou som,"   and a side feccheþ
Of þe barn þat ȝo bare,   and alle hire blode chaungeþ.

Forþ þey went for wo   wepande sore
And sayn, "alas in þis lif   how longe schul we dwelle?
Ȝit beter were at o brayde   in batail to deye
1100 Þan þus in langur to lyue   and lengþen our fyne."

One Mary, a mild woman, because of absence of food,
Cooked on the coals her own baby, whom she bore.
She roasts the spine and the ribs, with pitiful words,
Says: "Son, upon each side is our sorrow increased:

Battle is outside the city to slaughter our bodies,   1085
Hunger is so hot within that our hearts nearly burst.
Therefore give up what I gave you, and turn back again,
Enter where you came out"—and she eats a shoulder.

Then the smell of the roast rose into the street,
So that many starving people smelled the aroma.   1090
They bashed down the door: the woman must die
Who in this misfortune concealed meat from men.

Then the worthy woman says, in a wild hunger:
"I have cooked my own baby and gnawed on the bones,
But I have saved some for you." And she fetches a side   1095
Of the baby, whom she bore—and all their blood changes.

They walked away weeping bitterly for woe,
And saying: "Alas! How long shall we dwell in this life?
It is better yet to die in an instant in battle
Than to live on thus in misery and lengthen our end."   1100

B. *The Siege of Jerusalem* and the Bible: Key Passages

The most important narratives shaping *The Siege of Jerusalem*, as its Prologue makes especially clear, are biblical. The poet incorporates many biblical allusions and quotations, and he expected an audience who knew the biblical foundations that informed his Christian interpretation of the destruction of the Second Temple. Especially important contexts are the history of the Jewish Maccabean Revolt as told in 1 and 2 Maccabees; the story of the betrayal, trial, and crucifixion of Jesus as told in the four gospels; and New Testament prophecies about the destruction and renewal of Jerusalem. Key passages are included here from the Douay-Rheims Bible, a Catholic English translation first published between 1582 and 1610, made from the Latin Vulgate (the common form of the medieval Bible) that the *Siege* poet would have used and known well.

1. 1 Maccabees 6 (Judas Maccabeus defends Jerusalem)

1 Maccabees is biblical apocrypha, that is, one of the books of the Christian Old Testament that is not part of the canon of Hebrew scripture and whose authority has therefore been debated over the centuries. The late-fourteenth-century *Siege of Jerusalem* poet would have considered it scriptural, among the historical books that tell of the divine path of God's chosen people, Israel. It tells the story of Jewish revolt against Seleucid rulers, Greek kings who ruled over the empire created by the conquests of Alexander the Great, and the origins of the Jewish Hasmonean dynasty that ruled in Judea c. 140–116 BCE. The Seleucid king Antiochus IV Epiphanes had attacked Jerusalem in 167 BCE, killing many Jews, forbidding Jewish religious rites, and desecrating the Temple. This attack gave rise to a rebellion led by Judas Maccabeus (or "Judah the Hammer"), a pious Jew who fought against Seleucids and Hellenized Jews to regain autonomous Jewish rights and the governorship of Jerusalem and Judea. Chapter 6, excerpted below, describes events around the death of Antiochus IV, including the Maccabean forces' defense of Jerusalem and other Judean fortifica-

tions. The author of 1 Maccabees regards the rebels as heroic and the Seleucids and Hellenized Jews as capricious and perfidious.

1 Now king Antiochus[1] was going through the higher countries, and he heard that the city of Elymais in Persia was greatly renowned and abounding in silver and gold.

2 And that there was in it a temple exceeding rich and coverings of gold and breastplates and shields which king Alexander,[2] son of Philip the Macedonian that reigned first in Greece, had left there.

3 Lo, he came and sought to take the city and to pillage it: but he was not able, because the design was known to them that were in the city.

4 And they rose up against him in battle: and he fled away from thence and departed with great sadness and returned towards Babylonia.

5 And whilst he was in Persia, there came one that told him, how the armies that were in the land of Juda were put to flight:

6 And that Lysias[3] went with a very great power and was put to flight before the face of the Jews: and that they were grown strong by the armour and power and store of spoils which they had gotten out of the camps which they had destroyed:

7 And that they had thrown down the abomination[4] which he had set up upon the altar in Jerusalem, and that they had compassed about the sanctuary with high walls as before, and Bethsura[5] also his city.

8 And it came to pass when the king heard these words, that he was struck with fear and exceedingly moved. And he laid himself down upon his bed and fell sick for grief, because it had not fallen out to him as he imagined.

9 And he remained there many days: for great grief came more and more upon him, and he made account that he should die.

---

1   *Antiochus*   Antiochus IV Epiphanes, Seleucid king c. 215–164 BCE.
2   *Alexander*   Alexander the Great.
3   *Lysias*   Seleucid general and governor of Syria.
4   *abomination*   Statue of a pagan god, a desecration of the Temple committed after Antiochus IV's previous assault on Jerusalem.
5   *Bethsura*   Beth-zur, about 20 miles south of Jerusalem.

10 And he called for all his friends and said to them: Sleep is gone from my eyes, and I am fallen away, and my heart is cast down for anxiety.

11 And I said in my heart: Into how much tribulation am I come, and into what floods of sorrow, wherein now I am: I that was pleasant and beloved in my power!

12 But now I remember the evils that I have done in Jerusalem, from whence also I took away all the spoils of gold and of silver that were in it, and I sent to destroy the inhabitants of Juda without cause.

13 I know therefore that for this cause these evils have found me: and behold I perish with great grief in a strange land.

14 Then he called Philip, one of his friends: and he made him regent over all his kingdom.

15 And he gave him the crown and his robe and his ring, that he should go to Antiochus his son and should bring him up for the kingdom.

16 So king Antiochus died there in the year one hundred and forty-nine.[1]

17 And Lysias understood that the king was dead: and he set up Antiochus his son to reign, whom he brought up young: and he called his name Eupator.

18 Now they that were in the castle[2] had shut up the Israelites round about the holy places: and they were continually seeking their hurt and to strengthen the Gentiles.

19 And Judas purposed to destroy them:[3] and he called together all the people, to besiege them.

20 And they came together, and besieged them in the year one hundred and fifty:[4] and they made battering slings and engines.

21 And some of the besieged got out: and some wicked men of Israel[5] joined themselves unto them.

22 And they went to the king[6] and said: How long dost thou delay to execute the judgment and to revenge our brethren?

---

1 *one hundred and forty-nine*   164 BCE. The author uses the Seleucid-Macedonian calendar.

2 *they that ... the castle*   Seleucid garrison inside the citadel at Jerusalem.

3 *Judas ... to destroy them*   I.e., Judas Maccabeus plotted to destroy the Seleucid garrison.

4 *one hundred and fifty*   163 or 162 BCE.

5 *wicked men of Israel*   Hellenized, pro-Seleucid Jews.

6 *the king*   Now Antiochus V Eupator, who ruled 163–161 BCE.

23 We determined to serve thy father and to do according to his orders and obey his edicts:

24 And for this they of our nation are alienated from us and have slain as many of us as they could find and have spoiled our inheritances.[1]

25 Neither have they put forth their hand against us only but also against all our borders.

26 And behold they have approached this day to the castle of Jerusalem to take it and they have fortified the stronghold of Bethsura.

27 And unless thou speedily prevent them, they will do greater things than these, and thou shalt not be able to subdue them.

28 Now when the king heard this, he was angry: and he called together all his friends and the captains of his army and them that were over the horsemen.

29 There came also to him from other realms and from the islands of the sea hired troops.

30 And the number of his army was an hundred thousand footmen and twenty thousand horsemen and thirty-two elephants, trained to battle.

31 And they went through Idumea[2] and approached to Bethsura and fought many days: and they made engines. But they sallied forth and burnt them with fire and fought manfully.

32 And Judas departed from the castle and removed the camp to Bethzacharam,[3] over against the king's camp.

33 And the king rose before it was light and made his troops march on fiercely towards the way of Bethzacharam. And the armies made themselves ready for the battle: and they sounded the trumpets.

34 And they showed the elephants the blood of grapes and mulberries, to provoke them to fight.

35 And they distributed the beasts by the legions: and there stood by every elephant a thousand men in coats of mail and with helmets of brass on their heads: and five hundred horsemen set in order were chosen for every beast.

---

1 *our nation are alienated ... inheritances* Maccabean rebels considered Jews who accepted Seleucid rule apostates.
2 *Idumea* Biblical kingdom of Edom, south of Judea.
3 *Bethzacharam* Beth-zechariah, 10 miles southwest of Jerusalem.

36 These before the time, wheresoever the beast was, they were there: and whithersoever it went, they went: and they departed not from it.

37 And upon the beast there were strong wooden towers which covered every one of them, and engines upon them: and upon every one thirty-two valiant men, who fought from above, and an Indian to rule the beast.

38 And the rest of the horsemen he[1] placed on this side and on that side at the two wings, with trumpets to stir up the army and to hasten them forward that stood thick together in the legions thereof.

39 Now when the sun shone upon the shields of gold and of brass, the mountains glittered therewith: and they shone like lamps of fire.

40 And part of the king's army was distinguished by the high mountains, and the other part by the low places: and they marched on warily and orderly.

41 And all the inhabitants of the land were moved at the noise of their multitude and the marching of the company and the rattling of the armour, for the army was exceeding great and strong.

42 And Judas and his army drew near for battle: and there fell of the king's army six hundred men.

43 And Eleazar the son of Saura[2] saw one of the beasts harnessed with the king's harness: and it was higher than the other beasts. And it seemed to him that the king was on it.

44 And he exposed himself to deliver his people and to get himself an everlasting name.

45 And he ran up to it boldly in the midst of the legion, killing on the right hand and on the left: and they fell by him on this side and that side.

46 And he went between the feet of the elephant and put himself under it and slew it: and it fell to the ground upon him, and he died there.

47 Then they, seeing the strength of the king and the fierceness of his army, turned away from them.

48 But the king's army went up against them to Jerusalem: and the king's army pitched their tents against Judea and Mount Sion.[3]

---

1 *he* Antiochus V Eupator.

2 *Eleazar the son of Saura* Eleazar Avaran, younger brother of Judas Maccabeus.

3 *Mount Sion* I.e., the area around the Temple.

49 And he made peace with them that were in Bethsura. And they came forth out of the city, because they had no victuals, being shut up there: for it was the year of rest to the land.[1]

50 And the king took Bethsura: and he placed there a garrison to keep it.

51 And he turned his army against the sanctuary[2] for many days: and he set up there battering slings and engines and instruments to cast fire and engines to cast stones and javelins and pieces to shoot arrows, and slings.

52 And they also made engines against their engines: and they fought for many days.

53 But there were no victuals in the city, because it was the seventh year: and such as had stayed in Judea of them that came from among the nations[3] had eaten the residue of all that which had been stored up.

54 And there remained in the holy places but a few, for the famine had prevailed over them: and they were dispersed every man to his own place.[4]

55 Now Lysias heard that Philip, whom king Antiochus while he lived had appointed to bring up his son Antiochus, and to reign, to be king,

56 Was returned from Persia and Media, with the army that went with him and that he sought to take upon him the affairs of the kingdom.

57 Wherefore he made haste to go and say to the king[5] and to the captains of the army: We decay daily and our provision of victuals is small and the place that we lay siege to is strong: and it lieth upon us to take order for the affairs of the kingdom.

58 Now therefore let us come to an agreement with these men and make peace with them and with all their nation.[6]

---

1   *he made peace … rest to the land*   I.e., Antiochus V is able to retake Beth-zur, in part because the fallow year meant that the rebels had few supplies. The land was kept fallow every seven years.

2   *against the sanctuary*   Against the Temple at Jerusalem.

3   *such as had … among the nations*   Refugees evacuated to Judea because of conflicts.

4   *for the famine … own place*   I.e., the fallow year made prolonged conflict in both Beth-zur and Jerusalem impossible.

5   *he made haste … the king*   Lysias, nervous that Philip will take control, goes to Antiochus V.

6   *them and with all their nation*   The Maccabees and all Jews.

59 And let us covenant with them, that they may live according to their own laws as before. For because of our despising their laws, they have been provoked and have done all these things.

60 And the proposal was acceptable in the sight of the king and of the princes: and he sent to them to make peace: and they accepted of it.

61 And the king and the princes swore to them: and they came out of the stronghold.

62 Then the king entered into Mount Sion and saw the strength of the place: and he quickly broke the oath that he had taken and gave commandment to throw down the wall round about.

63 And he departed in haste and returned to Antioch, where he found Philip master of the city: and he fought against him and took the city.

2. The Gospel According to Matthew 10.1–15 (Jesus instructs the apostles and predicts destruction for the city that rejects them)

1 And having called his twelve disciples together, he gave them power over unclean spirits, to cast them out and to heal all manner of diseases and all manner of infirmities.

2 And the names of the twelve apostles are these: The first, Simon who is called Peter, and Andrew his brother.

3 James the son of Zebedee and John his brother, Philip and Bartholomew, Thomas and Matthew the publican, and James the son of Alpheus, and Thaddeus,

4 Simon the Cananean and Judas Iscariot, who also betrayed him.

5 These twelve Jesus sent, commanding them, saying: Go ye not into the way of the Gentiles and into the city of the Samaritans enter ye not.

6 But go ye rather to the lost sheep of the house of Israel.

7 And going, preach, saying: The kingdom of heaven is at hand.

8 Heal the sick, raise the dead, cleanse the lepers, cast out devils. Freely have you received: freely give.

9 Do not possess gold, nor silver, nor money in your purses,

10 Nor scrip for your journey, nor two coats, nor shoes, nor a staff. For the workman is worthy of his meat.

11 And into whatsoever city or town you shall enter, inquire who in it is worthy, and there abide till you go thence.

12 And when you come into the house, salute it, saying: Peace be to this house.

13 And if that house be worthy, your peace shall come upon it. But if it be not worthy, your peace shall return to you.

14 And whosoever shall not receive you, nor hear your words: going forth out of that house or city shake off the dust from your feet.

15 Amen I say to you, it shall be more tolerable for the land of Sodom and Gomorrha in the day of judgment than for that city.

3. The Gospel According to Matthew 26.14–15 and 27.1–9 (Judas Iscariot's betrayal and death)

26.14 Then went one of the twelve, who was called Judas Iscariot, to the chief priests,

15 And said to them: What will you give me, and I will deliver him unto you? But they appointed him thirty pieces of silver.

[…]

27.1 And when morning was come, all the chief priests and ancients of the people took counsel against Jesus, that they might put him to death.

2 And they brought him bound and delivered him to Pontius Pilate the governor.

3 Then Judas, who betrayed him, seeing that he was condemned, repenting himself, brought back the thirty pieces of silver to the chief priests and ancients,

4 Saying: I have sinned in betraying innocent blood. But they said: What is that to us? Look thou to it.

5 And casting down the pieces of silver in the temple, he departed and went and hanged himself with an halter.

6 But the chief priests having taken the pieces of silver, said: It is not lawful to put them into the corbona,[1] because it is the price of blood.

7 And after they had consulted together, they bought with them the potter's field, to be a burying place for strangers.

---

1 *corbona* The offering place in the Temple.

8 For this cause the field was called Haceldama, that is, The field of blood, even to this day.

9 Then was fulfilled that which was spoken by Jeremias the prophet, saying: And they took the thirty pieces of silver, the price of him that was prized, whom they prized of the children of Israel.[1]

4. The Gospel According to Luke 19.37–48 and 21.5–28 (Jesus enters Jerusalem and laments its destruction, the signs that will precede the destruction of Jerusalem and the end of days)

19.37 And when he was now coming near the descent of Mount Olivet,[2] the whole multitude of his disciples began with joy to praise God with a loud voice, for all the mighty works they had seen,

38 Saying: Blessed be the king who cometh in the name of the Lord! Peace in heaven and glory on high!

39 And some of the Pharisees,[3] from amongst the multitude, said to him: Master, rebuke thy disciples.[4]

40 To whom he said: I say to you that if these shall hold their peace, the stones will cry out.

41 And when he drew near, seeing the city, he wept over it, saying:

42 If thou[5] also hadst known, and that in this thy day, the things that are to thy peace: but now they are hidden from thy eyes.

43 For the days shall come upon thee: and thy enemies shall cast a trench about thee and compass thee round and straiten thee on every side,

44 And beat thee flat to the ground, and thy children who are in thee. And they shall not leave in thee a stone upon a stone: because thou hast not known the time of thy visitation.

45 And entering into the temple, he began to cast out them that sold therein and them that bought.

46 Saying to them: It is written: My house is the house of prayer.[6] But you have made it a den of thieves.

---

1 *Jeremias the prophet ... of Israel* Actually refers to Zechariah 11.12–13.
2 *Mount Olivet* Just east of Jerusalem.
3 *Pharisees* Jewish authorities.
4 *rebuke thy disciples* For acting as though Jesus is the Messiah.
5 *thou* Jerusalem.
6 *It is written ... of prayer* Isaiah 56.7.

47 And he was teaching daily in the temple. And the chief priests and the scribes[1] and the rulers of the people sought to destroy him.

48 And they found not what to do to him: for all the people were very attentive to hear him.

[...]

21.5 And some saying of the temple that it was adorned with goodly stones and gifts, he[2] said:

6 These things which you see, the days will come in which there shall not be left a stone upon a stone that shall not be thrown down.

7 And they asked him, saying: Master, when shall these things be? and what shall be the sign when they shall begin to come to pass?

8 Who said: Take heed you be not seduced; for many will come in my name, saying: I am he and the time is at hand. Go ye not therefore after them.

9 And when you shall hear of wars and seditions, be not terrified. These things must first come to pass: but the end is not yet presently.

10 Then he said to them: Nation shall rise against nation, and kingdom against kingdom.

11 And there shall be great earthquakes in divers places and pestilences and famines and terrors from heaven: and there shall be great signs.

12 But before all these things, they will lay their hands upon you and persecute you, delivering you up to the synagogues and into prisons, dragging you before kings and governors, for my name's sake.

13 And it shall happen unto you for a testimony.

14 Lay it up therefore into your hearts, not to meditate before how you shall answer:

15 For I will give you a mouth and wisdom, which all your adversaries shall not be able to resist and gainsay.

16 And you shall be betrayed by your parents and brethren and kinsmen and friends: and some of you they will put to death.

17 And you shall be hated by all men for my name's sake.

18 But a hair of your head shall not perish.

19 In your patience you shall possess your souls.

---

1   *chief priests and the scribes*   Jewish religious authorities.
2   *he*   Jesus.

20 And when you shall see Jerusalem compassed about with an army, then know that the desolation thereof is at hand.

21 Then let those who are in Judea flee to the mountains: and those who are in the midst thereof, depart out: and those who are in the countries, not enter into it.

22 For these are the days of vengeance, that all things may be fulfilled, that are written.

23 But woe to them that are with child and give suck in those days: for there shall be great distress in the land and wrath upon this people.

24 And they shall fall by the edge of the sword and shall be led away captives into all nations: and Jerusalem shall be trodden down by the Gentiles[1] till the times of the nations be fulfilled.

25 And there shall be signs in the sun and in the moon and in the stars; and upon the earth distress of nations, by reason of the confusion of the roaring of the sea and of the waves:

26 Men withering away for fear and expectation of what shall come upon the whole world. For the powers of heaven shall be moved.

27 And then they shall see the Son of man coming in a cloud, with great power and majesty.

28 But when these things begin to come to pass, look up and lift up your heads, because your redemption is at hand.

5. The Gospel According to Luke 22.63–23.38 (Trial and crucifixion of Jesus)

22.63 And the men that held him mocked him and struck him.

64 And they blindfolded him and smote his face. And they asked him, saying: Prophesy, who is it that struck thee?

65 And blaspheming, many other things they said against him.

66 And as soon as it was day, the ancients of the people and the chief priests and scribes came together. And they brought him into their council, saying: If thou be the Christ, tell us.

67 And he saith to them: If I shall tell you, you will not believe me.

68 And if I shall also ask you, you will not answer me, nor let me go.

---

1   *Gentiles*   Non-Jewish nations.

69 But hereafter the Son of man shall be sitting on the right hand of the power of God.

70 Then said they all: Art thou then the Son of God? Who said: You say that I am.

71 And they said: What need we any further testimony? for we ourselves have heard it from his own mouth.

23.1 And the whole multitude of them, rising up, led him to Pilate.

2 And they began to accuse him, saying: We have found this man perverting our nation and forbidding to give tribute to Caesar and saying that he is Christ the king.

3 And Pilate asked him, saying: Art thou the king of the Jews? But he answering, said: Thou sayest it.

4 And Pilate said to the chief priests and to the multitudes: I find no cause in this man.[1]

5 But they were more earnest, saying: He stirreth up the people, teaching throughout all Judea, beginning from Galilee to this place.

6 But Pilate hearing Galilee, asked if the man were of Galilee?

7 And when he understood that he was of Herod's jurisdiction, he sent him away to Herod, who was also himself at Jerusalem in those days.

8 And Herod seeing Jesus, was very glad: for he was desirous of a long time to see him, because he had heard many things of him; and he hoped to see some sign wrought by him.

9 And he questioned him in many words. But he answered him nothing.

10 And the chief priests and the scribes stood by, earnestly accusing him.

11 And Herod with his army set him at nought[2] and mocked him, putting on him a white garment: and sent him back to Pilate.

12 And Herod and Pilate were made friends, that same day: for before they were enemies one to another.

13 And Pilate, calling together the chief priests and the magistrates and the people,

---

1 *no cause in this man* I.e., no reason to condemn him.
2 *set him at nought* Treated him as nothing, disgraced him.

14 Said to them: You have presented unto me this man as one that perverteth the people. And behold I, having examined him before you, find no cause in this man, in those things wherein you accuse him.

15 No, nor Herod neither. For, I sent you to him: and behold, nothing worthy of death is done to him.

16 I will chastise him therefore and release him.

17 Now of necessity he was to release unto them one upon the feast day.[1]

18 But the whole multitude together cried out, saying: Away with this man, and release unto us Barabbas:

19 Who, for a certain sedition made in the city and for a murder, was cast into prison.

20 And Pilate again spoke to them, desiring to release Jesus.

21 But they cried again, saying: Crucify him, Crucify him.

22 And he said to them the third time: Why, what evil hath this man done? I find no cause of death in him. I will chastise him therefore and let him go.

23 But they were instant with loud voices, requiring that he might be crucified. And their voices prevailed.

24 And Pilate gave sentence that it should be as they required.

25 And he released unto them him who for murder and sedition had been cast into prison, whom they had desired. But Jesus he delivered up to their will.

26 And as they led him away, they laid hold of one Simon of Cyrene, coming from the country; and they laid the cross on him to carry after Jesus.

27 And there followed him a great multitude of people and of women, who bewailed and lamented him.

28 But Jesus turning to them, said: Daughters of Jerusalem, weep not over me; but weep for yourselves and for your children.

29 For behold, the days shall come, wherein they will say: Blessed are the barren and the wombs that have not borne and the paps[2] that have not given suck.

30 Then shall they begin to say to the mountains: Fall upon us. And to the hills: Cover us.[3]

---

1   *he was to release ... feast day*   Pilate was to release a prisoner to the Jews at Passover.

2   *paps*   Breasts.

3   *Then shall ... Cover us*   Cf. Hosea 10.8.

31 For if in the green wood they do these things, what shall be done in the dry?

32 And there were also two other malefactors led with him to be put to death.

33 And when they were come to the place which is called Calvary, they crucified him there: and the robbers, one on the right hand, and the other on the left.

34 And Jesus said: Father, forgive them, for they know not what they do. But they, dividing his garments, cast lots.[1]

35 And the people stood beholding, and the rulers with them derided him, saying: He saved others: let him save himself, if he be Christ, the elect of God.

36 And the soldiers also mocked him, coming to him and offering him vinegar,

37 And saying: If thou be the king of the Jews, save thyself.

38 And there was also a superscription written over him in letters of Greek and Latin and Hebrew: THIS IS THE KING OF THE JEWS.

6. The Gospel According to John 11.47–53 and 18.3–19.22 (Council of the priests and Pharisees, arrest and crucifixion of Jesus)

11.47 The chief priests, therefore, and the Pharisees gathered a council[2] and said: What do we, for this man doth many miracles?

48 If we let him alone so, all will believe in him; and the Romans will come, and take away our place and nation.

49 But one of them, named Caiphas, being the high priest that year, said to them: You know nothing.

50 Neither do you consider that it is expedient for you that one man should die for the people and that the whole nation perish not.

51 And this he spoke not of himself: but being the high priest of that year, he prophesied that Jesus should die for the nation.

52 And not only for the nation, but to gather together in one the children of God that were dispersed.

53 From that day therefore they devised to put him to death.

[...]

---

1 *dividing his garments, cast lots*   Cf. Psalm 22.16–18.
2 *a council*   The Sanhedrin, the official Jewish court.

18.3 Judas[1] therefore having received a band of soldiers and servants from the chief priests and the Pharisees, cometh thither with lanterns and torches and weapons.

4 Jesus therefore, knowing all things that should come upon him, went forth and said to them: Whom seek ye?

5 They answered him: Jesus of Nazareth. Jesus saith to them: I am he. And Judas also, who betrayed him, stood with them.

6 As soon therefore as he had said to them: I am he; they went backward, and fell to the ground.

7 Again therefore he asked them: Whom seek ye? And they said: Jesus of Nazareth.

8 Jesus answered: I have told you that I am he. If therefore you seek me, let these[2] go their way,

9 That the word might be fulfilled which he said: Of them whom thou hast given me, I have not lost any one.[3]

10 Then Simon Peter, having a sword, drew it and struck the servant of the high priest and cut off his right ear. And the name of the servant was Malchus.

11 Jesus therefore said to Peter: Put up thy sword into the scabbard. The chalice which my Father hath given me, shall I not drink it?

12 Then the band and the tribune and the servants of the Jews took Jesus and bound him:

13 And they led him away to Annas first, for he was father-in-law to Caiphas, who was the high priest of that year.

14 Now Caiphas was he who had given the counsel to the Jews: That it was expedient that one man should die for the people.

[...]

19 The high priest therefore asked Jesus of his disciples and of his doctrine.

20 Jesus answered him: I have spoken openly to the world. I have always taught in the synagogue and in the temple, whither all the Jews resort: and in secret I have spoken nothing.

---

1 *Judas* Judas Iscariot.
2 *these* The apostles, who are with Jesus when he is arrested.
3 *the word ... lost any one* Cf. John 17.12.

21 Why asketh thou me? Ask them who have heard what I have spoken unto them. Behold they know what things I have said.

22 And when he had said these things, one of the servants standing by gave Jesus a blow, saying: Answerest thou the high priest so?

23 Jesus answered him: If I have spoken evil, give testimony of the evil; but if well, why strikest thou me?

24 And Annas sent him bound to Caiphas the high priest.

[...]

28 Then they led Jesus from Caiphas to the governor's[1] hall. And it was morning: and they went not into the hall, that they might not be defiled, but that they might eat the pasch.[2]

29 Pilate therefore went out to them, and said: What accusation bring you against this man?

30 They answered and said to him: If he were not a malefactor, we would not have delivered him up to thee.

31 Pilate therefore said to them: Take him you, and judge him according to your law. The Jews therefore said to him: It is not lawful for us to put any man to death.

32 That the word of Jesus might be fulfilled, which he said, signifying what death he should die.[3]

33 Pilate therefore went into the hall again and called Jesus and said to him: Art thou the king of the Jews?

34 Jesus answered: Sayest thou this thing of thyself, or have others told it thee of me?

35 Pilate answered: Am I a Jew? Thy own nation and the chief priests have delivered thee up to me. What hast thou done?

36 Jesus answered: My kingdom is not of this world. If my kingdom were of this world, my servants would certainly strive that I should not be delivered to the Jews: but now my kingdom is not from hence.

37 Pilate therefore said to him: Art thou a king then? Jesus answered: Thou sayest that I am a king. For this was I born, and for this

---

1 *the governor's* Pontius Pilate's.

2 *they went not ... eat the pasch* The Jewish authorities will not enter a Gentile home, lest they be made ritually unclean and therefore unable to eat the Passover meal.

3 *word of Jesus ... should die* Cf. John 12.32–33.

came I into the world; that I should give testimony to the truth. Every one that is of the truth heareth my voice.

38 Pilate saith to him: What is truth? And when he said this, he went out again to the Jews and saith to them: I find no cause in him.

39 But you have a custom that I should release one unto you at the pasch. Will you, therefore, that I release unto you the king of the Jews?

40 Then cried they all again, saying: Not this man, but Barabbas. Now Barabbas was a robber.

19.1 Then therefore Pilate took Jesus and scourged him.

2 And the soldiers platting a crown of thorns, put it upon his head: and they put on him a purple garment.

3 And they came to him and said: Hail, king of the Jews. And they gave him blows.

4 Pilate therefore went forth again and saith to them: Behold, I bring him forth unto you, that you may know that I find no cause in him.

5 (Jesus therefore came forth, bearing the crown of thorns and the purple garment.) And he[1] saith to them: Behold the Man.

6 When the chief priests, therefore, and the servants had seen him, they cried out, saying: Crucify him, Crucify him. Pilate saith to them: Take him you, and crucify him: for I find no cause in him.

7 The Jews answered him: We have a law; and according to the law he ought to die, because he made himself the Son of God.[2]

8 When Pilate therefore had heard this saying, he feared the more.

9 And he entered into the hall again; and he said to Jesus: Whence art thou? But Jesus gave him no answer.

10 Pilate therefore saith to him: Speakest thou not to me? Knowest thou not that I have power to crucify thee, and I have power to release thee?

11 Jesus answered: Thou shouldst not have any power against me, unless it were given thee from above. Therefore, he that hath delivered me to thee[3] hath the greater sin.

---

1 *he* Pilate.
2 *he made himself the Son of God* A blasphemy. See Leviticus 24.16.
3 *he that ... me to thee* Caiaphas.

12 And from henceforth Pilate sought to release him. But the Jews cried out, saying: If thou release this man, thou art not Caesar's friend. For whosoever maketh himself a king speaketh against Caesar.

13 Now when Pilate had heard these words, he brought Jesus forth, and sat down in the judgment seat, in the place that is called Lithostrotos,[1] and in Hebrew Gabbatha.

14 And it was the parasceve of the pasch,[2] about the sixth hour: and he saith to the Jews: Behold your king.

15 But they cried out: Away with him: Away with him: Crucify him. Pilate saith to them: Shall I crucify your king? The chief priests answered: We have no king but Caesar.

16 Then therefore he delivered him to them to be crucified. And they took Jesus and led him forth.

17 And bearing his own cross, he went forth to that place which is called Calvary, but in Hebrew Golgotha.

18 Where they crucified him, and with him two others, one on each side, and Jesus in the midst.

19 And Pilate wrote a title also, and he put it upon the cross. And the writing was: JESUS OF NAZARETH, THE KING OF THE JEWS.

20 This title therefore many of the Jews did read: because the place where Jesus was crucified was nigh to the city. And it was written in Hebrew, in Greek, and in Latin.

21 Then the chief priests of the Jews said to Pilate: Write not: The King of the Jews. But that he said: I am the King of the Jews.

22 Pilate answered: What I have written, I have written.

7. Revelation 21 (Vision of the new Jerusalem)

1 And I saw a new heaven and a new earth. For the first heaven and the first earth was gone: and the sea is now no more.

2 And I, John,[3] saw the holy city, the new Jerusalem, coming down out of heaven from God, prepared as a bride adorned for her husband.

---

1   *Lithostrotos*   Greek: the stone pavement.
2   *parasceve of the pasch*   Day before Passover.
3   *I, John*   Author of the apocalyptic book of Revelation, who reports that he received his visions from God while in exile on the island of Patmos (see Revelation 1.1–11). It is likely that Revelation was written after the destruction of Jerusalem in 70 CE, perhaps during the reign of Domitian (81–96 CE), Titus' younger brother.

3 And I heard a great voice from the throne, saying: Behold the tabernacle of God with men: and he will dwell with them. And they shall be his people: and God himself with them shall be their God.

4 And God shall wipe away all tears from their eyes: and death shall be no more. Nor mourning, nor crying, nor sorrow shall be any more: for the former things are passed away.

5 And he that sat on the throne, said: Behold, I make all things new. And he said to me: Write, for these words are most faithful and true.

6 And he said to me: It is done. I am Alpha and Omega: the Beginning and the End. To him that thirsteth, I will give of the fountain of the water of life, freely.

7 He that shall overcome shall possess these things, and I will be his God: and he shall be my son.

8 But the fearful and unbelieving and the abominable and murderers and whoremongers and sorcerers and idolaters and all liars, they shall have their portion in the pool burning with fire and brimstone, which is the second death.

9 And there came one of the seven angels, who had the vials full of the seven last plagues, and spoke with me, saying: Come and I will shew thee the bride, the wife of the Lamb.

10 And he took me up in spirit to a great and high mountain: and he shewed me the holy city Jerusalem coming down out of heaven from God,

11 Having the glory of God. And the light thereof was like to a precious stone, even as crystal.

12 And it had a wall great and high, having twelve gates, and in the gates twelve angels, and names written thereon, which are the names of the twelve tribes of the children of Israel.

13 On the east, three gates: and on the north, three gates: and on the south, three gates: and on the west, three gates.

14 And the wall of the city had twelve foundations: and in them, the twelve names of the twelve apostles of the Lamb.

15 And he that spoke with me had a measure of a reed of gold, to measure the city and the gates thereof and the wall.

16 And the city lieth in a foursquare: and the length thereof is as great as the breadth. And he measured the city with the golden reed

for twelve thousand furlongs: and the length and the height and the breadth thereof are equal.

17 And he measured the wall thereof, an hundred and forty-four cubits, the measure of a man, which is of an angel.

18 And the building of the wall thereof was of jasper stone: but the city itself pure gold, like to clear glass.

19 And the foundations of the wall of the city were adorned with all manner of precious stones. The first foundation was jasper: the second, sapphire: the third, a chalcedony: the fourth, an emerald:

20 The fifth, sardonyx: the sixth, sardius: the seventh, chrysolite: the eighth, beryl: the ninth, a topaz: the tenth, a chrysoprasus: the eleventh, a jacinth: the twelfth, an amethyst.

21 And the twelve gates are twelve pearls, one to each: and every several gate was of one several pearl. And the street of the city was pure gold, as it were, transparent glass.

22 And I saw no temple therein. For the Lord God Almighty is the temple thereof, and the Lamb.

23 And the city hath no need of the sun, nor of the moon, to shine in it. For the glory of God hath enlightened it: and the Lamb is the lamp thereof.

24 And the nations shall walk in the light of it: and the kings of the earth shall bring their glory and honour into it.

25 And the gates thereof shall not be shut by day: for there shall be no night there.

26 And they shall bring the glory and honour of the nations into it.

27 There shall not enter into it any thing defiled or that worketh abomination or maketh a lie: but they that are written in the book of life of the Lamb.

C. *The Siege of Jerusalem* and Medieval Christian Legend: Selections from *The Golden Legend* (c. 1260)

The Siege of Jerusalem, like many medieval works, freely intermingles pseudo-historical narratives, hagiography, and legend with biblical and historical information. The *Siege* poet evokes multiple genres of narrative and incorporates many types of sources. The result is an account of the destruction of the Second Temple that is a complex reworking of history—biblical, Roman, Jewish, and medieval—into a goal-oriented Christian narrative that reads history, backwards and forwards, as a matter of God's design.[1]

One of the poet's sources was a religious compilation known as the *Legenda aurea*, or *The Golden Legend*. The Latin *legenda* of the title means simply "readings" (literally, "things to be read") and carries few of the connotations that the Modern English word "legend" now does. The large collection was written in Latin sometime around 1260 CE by the Italian Dominican Jacobus de Voragine (later Archbishop of Genoa), and it contains nearly 200 readings on the lives of Christian saints and important biblical figures (such as Jesus, the apostles, and the Virgin Mary), and on important liturgical observances and celebrations (Christmas, Lent, Easter, etc.). *The Legend* was likely originally intended as a handbook of preaching material for clergy, but, by the *Siege* poet's time, it was widely read, both in private devotional and clerical use. As its twentieth-century translator William Granger Ryan summarizes, "The popularity of the *Legend* was such that some one thousand manuscripts have survived, and, with the advent of printing in the 1450s, editions in both the original Latin and in every Western European language multiplied into the hundreds. It has been said that in the late Middle Ages the only book more widely read was

---

1 For more on the poet's sources and influences, see the Introduction above.

the Bible."[1] The only known medieval translation into English was made in 1483, by the early printer William Caxton, and the *Siege* poet would have encountered it in Latin.

Included below are Modern English translations of sections of *The Golden Legend* that inform *The Siege of Jerusalem*. It is not necessarily the case that the poet had these items from *The Legend* at hand as he wrote, but it does seem that he knew these accounts well and presumed general knowledge of them on the part of his audience. As these excerpts will make clear, much of the related material from *The Legend* is itself a compilation of other, older sources (sometimes sources that the *Siege* poet also knew), but a few of the details of *The Siege of Jerusalem* do come directly from *The Legend*: the placement of Vespasian in Galatia and the nature of his illness (lines 33–40), the curing of Titus by Josephus during the siege (lines 1027–66), details of Nero's suicide (lines 903–20), and the length of the siege (line 1173). Most likely, however, is that these transferred details stem from deep familiarity rather than direct translation. *The Legend* is included here not only as one of the poet's sources, then, but also as a representative example of the kinds of hagiographical Christian narratives that informed him and many others in the period. What *The Golden Legend* tells us about the figures who appear in *Siege* is already the product of accreted Christian traditions and, as its author freely admits, includes contradictory sources. *The Legend* accumulates sources for the sake of argument, not necessarily prioritizing historical or factual accounts, and the method is instructional.

1. from "The Passion of the Lord"[2] (concerning Pilate and St. Veronica)

When Pilate had handed Jesus over to the Jews to be crucified, he was afraid that his condemnation of innocent blood might offend Tiberius Caesar, and dispatched one of his familiars to make a case for

---

1 From Ryan's introduction to his translation of Jacobus de Voragine, *The Golden Legend*, vol. 1 (Princeton: Princeton UP, 1993), xiii.

2 As translated by Ryan, *The Golden Legend*, vol. 1, 212-14. This excerpt is only indirectly related to *Siege*. It is clearly analogous to the poem, but it represents an older, distinct tradition. While the *Siege* poet may have included some details from it (Pilate's suicide and presence in Vienne, for example), it is more significant in this context as an available, competing narrative frame for the siege of Jerusalem story.

him to the emperor. Meanwhile, it was announced to Tiberius, who was seriously ill, that in Jerusalem there was a physician who cured all diseases by his word alone. Therefore the emperor, not knowing that Pilate and the Jews had put this physician to death, said to one of his intimates, whose name was Volusian: "Cross the sea as fast you can, and tell Pilate to send this healer to me so that he may restore me to health." Volusian came to Pilate and delivered the emperor's command, but Pilate, terror-stricken, asked for a fortnight's grace.

During this time Volusian made the acquaintance of a woman named Veronica, who had been in Jesus' company, and asked her where he might find Jesus Christ. She answered: "Alas, he was my Lord and my God, and Pilate, to whom he was handed over through envy, condemned him and commanded that he be crucified." Volusian was grieved at this and said: "I am deeply sorry that I cannot carry out the orders my master gave me." Veronica answered: "When the Teacher was going about preaching and I, to my regret, could not be with him, I wanted to have his picture painted so that when I was deprived of his presence, I could at least have the solace of his image. So one day I was carrying a piece of linen to the painter when I met Jesus, and he asked me where I was going. I told him what my errand was. He asked for the cloth I had in my hand, pressed it to his venerable face, and left his image on it. If your master looks devoutly upon this image, he will at once be rewarded by being cured." "Can this image be bought for gold or silver?" Volusian asked. "No," Veronica replied, "only true piety can make it effective. Therefore I will go with you and let Caesar look upon the image, after which I will return home." So Volusian came to Rome with Veronica and told Tiberius: "The Jesus you have long desired to see was unjustly given over to death by Pilate and the Jews, and, by reason of their envy, nailed to the gibbet of the cross. However, a lady came to me with a picture of Jesus, and if you look at it devoutly, you will obtain the benefit of your health." Caesar therefore had the road carpeted with silk cloths and ordered the image brought to him, and the moment he looked at it, he won back his pristine health.

Pontius Pilate was then taken prisoner at Caesar's command and shipped to Rome; and when the emperor heard that he had arrived, he was filled with fury and had him brought into his presence. Pilate, however, had taken with him the Lord's seamless tunic and came before the emperor wearing it. As soon as Tiberius saw him clothed in the tunic, his anger vanished. He rose to meet Pilate and could not address a harsh word to him. So the emperor, who, when Pilate was absent, seemed so terrible and furious, now, in his presence, was calmed. As soon as he had given him leave to go, on the other hand, he was again afire with rage and called himself a wretch for not having showed the culprit the anger that was in his heart. Swearing and protesting that Pilate was a son of death and that it was not right to let him live on the earth, he at once had him called back. But when he saw him, the emperor greeted him and his wrath subsided. All wondered, and he himself wondered, that he could be so wrought up against Pilate absent and could not so much as speak to him harshly when he was present. At length, at a sign from God, or perhaps a hint from some Christian, he had the man stripped of that tunic, and instantly his previous rage was rekindled. The emperor's astonishment mounted until he was told that the tunic had belonged to the Lord Jesus. He had Pilate remanded to prison until he could consult with a council of wise men about what should be done with the criminal. Pilate was forthwith sentenced to a shameful death, but when he heard of this, he killed himself with his own knife and so ended his life. When Caesar was informed of this, he said: "Truly he died a most shameful death, and his own hand did not spare him."[1]

The corpse was weighted with a huge stone and thrown into the Tiber, but wicked, foul spirits made sport of the wicked, foul body, plunging it into the water and snatching it up into the air. This caused awesome floods in the water and lightning, tempests, and hailstorms in the air, and a widespread panic broke out among the people. The Romans therefore pulled the body out of the Tiber and, as a gesture of contempt, carried it off to Vienne[2] and dumped it into the Rhone. The name of the city comes from *Via Gehennae*, the road to hell, because at that time it was a place of malediction. Or, more likely, the city was called Vienne or Bienna because it was said to have been built in a biennium. But there again the wicked spirits rallied and stirred up the same disturbances, and the people, refusing to put up with so great a plague of demons, removed that vessel of malediction

---

1 *Pilate was ... did not spare him* Cf. *Siege* lines 1327–34.
2 *Vienne* Cf. *Siege* line 1328.

from their midst and consigned it to burial in the territory of the city of Lausanne. There the populace, harried to excess by the aforesaid upheavals, took the body away and sank it in a pit surrounded by mountains, where, according to some accounts, diabolical machinations still make themselves felt.... Thus far we have quoted the aforementioned apocryphal history: let the reader judge whether the story is worth the telling.

It should be noted, however, that the *Scholastic History*[1] tells us that the Jews accused Pilate to Tiberius of the savage massacre of the Innocents,[2] of placing pagan images in the Temple despite the protests of the Jews, and of appropriating money taken from the corbona, or poor-chest, for his own uses such as building a water conduit into his house. For all these misdeeds he was deported into exile at Lyons, his city of origin, and there he died, despised by his own people. It could be, if there is any truth to this story, that Tiberius had decreed his exile and had had him deported to Lyons before Volusian came back to Rome from Jerusalem and reported to the emperor, but then, learning how he had put Christ to death, had the miscreant brought out of exile and returned to Rome. Neither Eusebius nor Bede[3] says in his chronicle that Pilate was exiled, but only that he suffered many calamities and died by his own hand.

---

1 *Scholastic History*   Peter Comestor's *Historia scholastica*, a late-twelfth-century Latin biblical compendium.

2 *massacre of the Innocents*   See Matthew 2.16–18.

3 *Eusebius ... Bede*   Eusebius (263–339 CE) was Bishop of Caesarea and author of one of the earliest narrative histories of the early Christian church, usually called the *Historia ecclesiastica*. Bede (?672–735 CE) was an English monk whose *Historia ecclesiastica gentis Anglorum* (*Ecclesiastical History of the English People*) was a model of national religious history for medieval writers.

2. from "Saint James, Apostle"[1] (concerning the death of St. James and the destruction of Jerusalem)

In the seventh year of his episcopate, when on Easter Sunday the apostles had gathered in Jerusalem, James[2] asked each of them how much the Lord had done among the people through them, and they gave their accounts. Then for seven days James and the other apostles preached in the Temple before Caiaphas and a number of Jews, and the time was at hand when they would have wished to be baptized. Suddenly a man came into the Temple and shouted: "O men of Israel, what are you doing? Why do you let these sorcerers delude us?" He stirred up the people so much that they wanted to stone the apostles. The man climbed up to the platform from which James was preaching and threw him to the floor below, and as a result James limped badly for the rest of his life. This happened to him in the seventh year after the Lord's ascension.

In the thirtieth year of his episcopate, the Jews, seeing that they could not kill Paul, who had appealed to Caesar and been sent to Rome, turned their tyrannical persecution on James. Hegesippus reports, as we find in the *Ecclesiastical History*,[3] that the Jews came together to him and said: "We pray you, call the people back, because they are wrong about Jesus, thinking that he is the Christ! We beg you therefore to speak to all these people who are coming for the day of the Pasch,[4] and to disabuse them about Jesus. We all will comply with what you say, and we, together with the people, will testify that you are a righteous man and that you are no respecter of persons." They stood him therefore on the pinnacle of the Temple and shouted: "Most righteous of men, to whom we all owe deference, the people are wrong in following Jesus who was crucified! Tell us plainly what you think about him!" James responded: "Why do you question me about the Son of man? Behold, he is seated in the heavens at the right

---

1 *"Saint James, Apostle"* As translated by Ryan, *The Golden Legend*, vol. 1, 271–77.

2 *James* Traditionally considered the first bishop of Jerusalem (based on Acts 15 and 21.17–18), mentioned in Siege at lines 1238–40.

3 *Hegesippus ... Ecclesiastical History* The work of Hegesippus, a second-century Christian historian, survives mainly through Eusebius's *Historia ecclesiastica*, to which Jacobus refers.

4 *Pasch* Passover.

of the sovereign Power, and he will come to judge the living and the dead!"

The Christians rejoiced at hearing this and listened to him gladly. The Pharisees and the Scribes said to each other: "We made a mistake in allowing him to give such testimony to Jesus! Now let us go up and throw him down! That will frighten this crowd and they won't dare believe what he said!" Then all together, and as loudly as they could, they shouted: "Oh! Oh! The just man has erred!"

Then they went up and threw him down, and came down again and began to stone him, saying: "Let us stone James the Just!" But James, though beaten to the ground, not only could not die but even turned over, raised himself to his knees, and said: "I pray you, Lord, forgive them, for they know not what they do!"[1] At this, one of the priests, of the sons of Rahab, exclaimed: "Stop! What are you doing? This just man whom you're stoning is praying for you!" But one of the others snatched up a fuller's club, aimed a heavy blow at James's head, and split his skull. That is how Hegesippus describes the martyrdom. James migrated to the Lord under Nero, who began to reign in the year of the Lord 57. He was buried there beside the Temple. The people were determined to avenge his death and capture and punish the malefactors, but these quickly got away.

Josephus says that the destruction of Jerusalem and the dispersion of the Jews were a punishment for the sin of killing James the Just. Jerusalem, however, was destroyed not only on account of James's death but especially on account of the death of the Lord,[2] according to what Christ himself said: "They will not leave one stone upon another in you, because you did not know the time of your visitation."[3]

But because the Lord does not wish the death of a sinner, and so that the Jews would have no excuse for their sin, he gave them forty years to do penance, and called upon them to do so through the apostles and especially through James the brother of the Lord, who continuously preached repentance among them. When no amount of admonition availed, God willed to terrify them with wonders. During

---

1   *"I pray you ... what they do!"* Cf. Luke 23.34.

2   *Josephus says ... of the Lord* Cf. *Siege* lines 1238–40, where the reasoning is similar. Michael Livingston (102) also reads line 724 as a reference to James.

3   *"They will not ... your visitation."* Cf. Luke 19.44, and the repetition of this gospel prophecy at *Siege* lines 355–56, 982, 1019–20, and 1289–92.

the forty years he had granted them for penance, many prodigies and portents occurred, as Josephus tells us. An extraordinarily brilliant star, similar in shape to a sword, hung over the city for a whole year, shooting out deadly flames. On a certain feast of Unleavened Bread,[1] at the ninth hour of the night a light shone around the altar of the Temple, so brilliant that all thought a marvelously bright day had dawned. On the same feast day a heifer that was already in the hands of the ministers to be sacrificed brought forth a lamb. Some days later, at the hour of sunset, cars and chariots were seen racing across every quarter of the sky, and battalions of armed men clashing in the clouds and surrounding the city with unlooked-for troops. On another feast day, which is called Pentecost,[2] the priests went at night to the Temple to conduct the usual ministries, and heard movements and crashing noises and voices saying: "Let us get away from this place!" And four years before the war, at the feast of Tabernacles,[3] a man by the name of Jesus, son of Ananias, suddenly began to shout: "A voice from the East, a voice from the West, a voice from the four winds, a voice over Jerusalem and over the Temple, a voice over husbands and wives, a voice over the whole people!" The man was caught, beaten, whipped, but could say nothing else, and the more he was whipped, the louder he shouted. He was brought before the judge, tortured, mangled until his bones showed through the torn flesh, but he neither begged nor wept, only howling at each blow and repeating the same words, adding: "Woe, woe to Jerusalem!" All this from Josephus.

The Jews were neither converted by admonitions nor frightened by marvels, so after forty years the Lord brought Vespasian and Titus to Jerusalem, and they razed the city to its foundations. The reason for their coming to Jerusalem is explained in a certain admittedly apocryphal history. There we read that Pilate, realizing that in Jesus he had condemned an innocent man and fearing the displeasure of Tiberius Caesar, sent an envoy named Albanus[4] to present his excuses to the emperor. Pilate's envoy was driven ashore in Galatia by contrary

---

1 *feast of Unleavened Bread* Passover.
2 *Pentecost* Not the Christian holiday but the Jewish holiday of Shavuot (50 days after Passover).
3 *feast of Tabernacles* Jewish holiday of Sukkot.
4 *Albanus* This envoy from Pilate is analogous to Nathan in the *Siege*, the product of another, parallel story in the Vengeance of Our Lord tradition.

winds and taken to Vespasian, who at that time held the governorship of Galatia[1] from Tiberius. The prevailing custom in that country was that anyone who had been shipwrecked had to give his goods and his service to the ruler. So Vespasian asked Albanus who he was, where he came from, and where he was going. Albanus answered: "I live in Jerusalem, that is where I came from, and I was on my way to Rome." Vespasian: "You come from the land of the wise men, you know the art of medicine, you are a physician! You must cure me!" In fact since childhood he had had some kind of worms in his nose, whence his name Vespasian. Albanus: "My lord, I know nothing of medicine and therefore am unable to cure you." Vespasian: "Cure me or die!" Albanus: "He who gave sight to the blind, drove out demons, and raised the dead, he knows that I have no knowledge of the art of healing." Vespasian: "Who is this that you say such great things about?" Albanus: "Jesus of Nazareth, whom the Jews, in their envy, put to death! If you believe in him you will obtain the grace of health." Vespasian: "I believe, because he who raised the dead will be able to free me of this ailment."

As he said this, the worms fell out of his nose and he received his health then and there. Filled with joy, he said: "I am sure that he who was able to cure me is the Son of God. I will seek permission of the emperor and go with an armed band to Jerusalem, and I will overthrow all those who betrayed and killed this man!" And Vespasian said to Albanus, Pilate's envoy: "Your life and goods are safe and unharmed, and you have my permission to return home."

Vespasian then went to Rome and obtained Tiberius Caesar's permission to destroy Jerusalem and Judea. For years during the reign of Nero, when the Jews were rebelling against the empire, he built up several armies: hence (according to the chronicles) he was acting not out of zeal for Christ but because the Jews were renouncing Roman rule. Vespasian then marched upon Jerusalem with a huge force, and on the day of the Pasch laid siege to the city and trapped the innumerable multitude gathered there for the festal day. Some time before Vespasian's arrival the Christian faithful who were in Jerusalem had been warned by the Holy Spirit to leave the city and to take refuge in a town called Pella, across the Jordan. Thus, with all her holy

---

1   *the governship of Galatia* Cf. *Siege* lines 39–40.

men withdrawn, Jerusalem became the place where the vengeance of heaven fell, upon the sacrilegious city and its people.

The Romans' first assault, however, was against a town of Judea called Jonapata,[1] in which Josephus was both leader and ruler, and he and his people put up a brave resistance; but at length Josephus, seeing that the city's fall was inevitable, took eleven Jews with him and sought safety in an underground room. After four days without food his associates, though Josephus disagreed, preferred to die there rather than submit to servitude under Vespasian. They wanted to kill each other and offer their blood in sacrifice to God; and, since Josephus held first rank among them, they thought he should be the first to die, so that by the shedding of his blood God would be the sooner placated. Or (as another chronicle has it) they wanted to kill each other so as not to fall into the hands of the Romans.

Now Josephus, being a prudent man and not wanting to die, appointed himself arbiter of death and sacrifice, and ordered the others to cast lots, two by two, to determine which of each pair would put the other to death. The lots were cast and one man after the other was consigned to death, until the last one was left to draw lots with Josephus. Then Josephus, who was a strong, agile man, took the other man's sword away from him, asked him which he preferred, life or death, and ordered him not to waste time choosing. The man, afraid, answered promptly: "I do not refuse to live, if by your favor I am able to save my life."

Josephus now had a talk in hiding with an intimate of Vespasian with whom he himself was on friendly terms: he requested that his life be spared by Vespasian, and what he requested he obtained. He was taken before Vespasian, who said to him: "You would have deserved death, if this man's petition had not secured your freedom!" Josephus: "If anything wrong has been done, it can be set right!" Vespasian: "What can a conquered man do?" Josephus: "I will be able to do something, if what I say wins me a favorable hearing." Vespasian: "It is granted that you may say what you have to say, and if there is any good in it, it will be listened to quietly." Josephus: "The Roman emperor has died, and the Senate has made you emperor!" Vespasian: "If you are a

---

1   *Jonapata*   I.e., Jotapata (north of Jerusalem), which fell to the Romans in 67 CE.

prophet, why did you not prophesy to this city that it was about to fall under my sway?" Josephus: "I foretold it publicly for forty days!"

Shortly thereafter legates arrived from Rome, affirmed that Vespasian had indeed been elevated to the imperial throne, and took him off to Rome. Eusebius, too, states in his chronicle that Josephus prophesied to Vespasian both about the emperor's death and about his own elevation.

Vespasian left his son Titus in charge of the siege of Jerusalem. We read in the same apocryphal history that Titus, hearing of his father's accession to the empire, was so filled with joy and exultation that he caught a chill and suffered a contraction of nerves and muscles that left him painfully paralyzed in one leg.[1] Josephus heard that Titus was paralyzed, and diligently sought information regarding the cause of the disease and the time it had struck. The cause was unknown, the nature of the illness also unknown, but the time was known: it happened to Titus when he learned of his father's election. Josephus, quick and foresighted as he was, put two and two together, and, knowing the time, surmised both the nature of the ailment and its cure. He knew that Titus had been debilitated by an excess of joy and gladness, and, keeping in mind that opposites are cured by opposites, knowing also that what is brought on by love is often dispelled by dislike, he began to ask whether there was anyone who was particularly obnoxious to the prince. There was indeed a slave who annoyed Titus so much that the very sight of him, and even the sound of his name, upset him completely. So Josephus said to Titus: "If you want to be cured, guarantee the safety of any who come in my company." Titus: "Whoever comes in your company will be kept secure and safe!"

Josephus quickly arranged a festive dinner, set his own table facing that of Titus, and seated the slave at his right side. When Titus saw the fellow, he growled with displeasure; and as he had been chilled by joy, he now was heated by his fit of fury: his sinews were loosened, and he was cured. Thereafter Titus granted his favor to the slave and took Josephus into his friendship. Whether this story is worth telling is left to the reader's judgment.

---

1   *so filled ... in one leg*   For this episode, cf. Titus and Josephus at *Siege* lines 1029–66.

Titus maintained the blockade of Jerusalem for two years.[1] Among the other ills that weighed heavily on the people in the besieged city, there was a famine so severe that parents snatched food from their children and children from parents, husbands from wives and wives from husbands—snatched it not only from their hands but out of their mouths. Young people, though stronger by their age, wandered about the streets like phantoms and fell down exhausted by hunger. Those who were burying the dead often fell dead on top of those they were burying. The stench from the cadavers was so unbearable that they were being buried out of public funds, and when the funds ran out, the unburied corpses were so numerous that they were thrown over the city walls. Titus, making a tour around the walls and seeing the moats filled with cadavers and the whole area infected with the smell of death, raised his hands to heaven, wept, and said: "God, you see that not I am doing this!"

The hunger was so acute that people chewed their shoes and their shoelaces. The *Ecclesiastical History*[2] tells the story of a woman noble by birth and by riches, whose house was broken into by robbers who stole all she had, including the last bit of food. She held her suckling infant in her hands and said: "Unhappy son of an unhappier mother, for whom should I keep you alive amid war and pillaging? Come now therefore, my firstborn, be food to your mother, a scandal to the robbers, a testament to the ages!" She strangled her child, cooked the body, ate half, and hid the other half.[3] The robbers, smelling cooked meat, rushed back into the house and threatened the woman with death unless she gave up the food. She uncovered what was left of the infant. "Look here," she said, "you see I saved you the best part!" But they were filled with such horror that they could not even speak. "This is my son," she said. "The sin is mine! Don't be afraid to eat, because I who begot him ate first. Don't be either more religious than the mother or more softhearted than women! But if piety overcomes

---

1   *two years* Cf. *Siege* lines 955 and 1173.
2   *Ecclesiastical History* Of Eusebius, who also made use of Josephus' eyewitness accounts of the siege.
3   *She strangled ... the other half* For this episode, cf. *Siege* lines 1081–1100, though *The Golden Legend* is likely not the direct source. The horrific cannibal-mother scene is a set-piece in historical and legendary accounts of the siege and was first recounted by Josephus in his *Wars of the Jews*. More information is included in the Introduction above.

you and you dread to eat, I will eat the rest, since I've already eaten half!" Trembling and terrified, the robbers slunk away.

Finally, in the second year of Vespasian's reign, Titus took Jerusalem, reduced the city to ruins, and leveled the Temple; and as the Jews had bought Jesus Christ for thirty pieces of silver, Titus had Jews sold at the rate of thirty for one silver coin.[1] Josephus tells us that 97,000 were sold and 111,000 perished of hunger or by the sword. We also read that when Titus entered the city, he noticed one particularly thick wall and gave orders to break into it. Inside the wall they found an old man, venerable in age and appearance. When asked who he was, he replied that he was Joseph, from Arimathea,[2] a city of Judea, and that the Jews had had him shut in and immured because he had buried Christ. He added that from that time to the present he had been fed with food from heaven and comforted by divine light. In the *Gospel of Nicodemus*,[3] however, it is said that though the Jews had walled him in, the risen Christ broke him out and brought him to Arimathea. It could be said that once released he would not desist from preaching Christ and therefore was walled in a second time.

Vespasian died and his son Titus succeeded him as emperor. He was a clement and generous man. His goodness was so great that, as Eusebius of Caesarea in his chronicle and Jerome[4] both affirm, when one evening he remembered that on that day he had done nothing good nor given anything to anyone, he said: "Oh, my friends, I have lost the day!"

Long afterwards some Jews set out to rebuild Jerusalem, and when they went out the first morning, they found crosses of dew on the ground. Frightened, they fled. The second morning they came back, and, as Miletus[5] says in his chronicle, each of them found a bloody

---

1 *as the Jews ... one silver coin* Cf. *Siege* lines 1161–72, though this episode is also found in multiple sources.

2 *Joseph, from Arimathea* A disciple of Jesus who removed his body from the cross and prepared it for interment. See Mark 15.43–46 and John 19.38.

3 *Gospel of Nicodemus* An important component text, also known as the *Acts of Pilate*, in the development of the Vengeance of Our Lord tradition. Extremely popular in the Middle Ages, it developed from the fourth century through the Middle Ages to include legendary accounts of the Crucifixion, the Harrowing of Hell, the reign of Tiberius, and the story of St. Veronica and her veil.

4 *Jerome* St. Jerome (347–420 CE), influential Christian historian and scholar, best known for his translation of the Bible into Latin (i.e., the Vulgate).

5 *Miletus* Hesychius of Miletus, sixth-century Greek historian.

cross sketched on his clothing. Again they fled in terror. When they returned on the third day, a fiery vapor came out of the ground and consumed them utterly.

3. from "Saint Peter, Apostle"[1] (concerning the deaths of St. Peter, St. Paul, and Nero)

Now [Peter] was taken prisoner by Nero's men and brought to the prefect Agrippa;[2] and, as Linus[3] says, his face shone like the sun. Agrippa said to him: "So you are the one who glories among the common people and the little women whom you wean from their husbands' beds!" But the apostle broke in to say that he gloried only in the cross of Jesus Christ. Then Peter, being an alien, was condemned to be crucified, while Paul, because he was a Roman citizen, was sentenced to beheading. Dionysius[4] wrote about this judgment scene in his letter to Timothy on the death of Saint Paul: "O my brother Timothy, if you had seen the way they were treated in their last hours, you would have fainted with sadness and grief. Who would not weep in that hour when the sentence came down that Peter was to be crucified and Paul to be beheaded! Then you would have seen the mob of pagans and Jews striking them and spitting in their faces! And when came the awful moment of their consummation, they were separated from each other, and these pillars of the world were put in chains as the brethren groaned and wept. Then Paul said to Peter: 'Peace be with you, foundation stone of the churches and shepherd of the sheep and lambs of Christ!' Peter said to Paul: 'Go in peace, preacher of virtuous living, mediator and leader of the salvation of the righteous!' When the two were taken away in different directions because they were not put to death in the same place, I followed my master." So Dionysius.

---

1 *"Saint Peter, Apostle"* As translated by Ryan, *The Golden Legend*, vol. 1, 344–48.

2 *Agrippa* King Herod Agrippa II.

3 *Linus* Linus of Rome, cited by Eusebius as a companion of Paul, perhaps the Linus mentioned in 2 Timothy 4.21.

4 *Dionysius* Dionysius the Areopagite, first-century convert to Christianity cited by Eusebius and in Acts 17.34. Letters attributed to him in the Middle Ages are generally recognized as the work of a sixth-century theologian now called Psuedo-Dionysius.

Pope Leo and Marcellus[1] assert that when Peter came to the cross, he said: "Because my Lord came down from heaven to earth, his cross was raised straight up; but he deigns to call me from earth to heaven, and my cross should have my head toward the earth and should point my feet toward heaven. Therefore, since I am not worthy to be on the cross the way my Lord was, turn my cross and crucify me head down!" So they turned the cross and nailed him to it with his feet upwards and his hands downwards. At the sight of this the people were enraged, and wanted to kill Nero and the prefect and free the apostle, but he pleaded with them not to hinder his martyrdom. Hegesippus and Linus say that the Lord opened the eyes of those who were weeping there, and they saw angels standing with crowns of roses and lilies, and Peter standing with them at the cross, receiving a book from Christ and reading from the book the words that he spoke.

[...]

On the day of their death Peter and Paul appeared to Dionysius, according to what he says in the aforementioned letter: "My brother Timothy, hear the miracle, see the marvel, of the day of their martyrdom! For I was present at the moment when they were separated: after their death I saw them coming in hand in hand at the gate of the city, clothed in luminous garments and crowned with crowns of brilliance and light." Thus Dionysius.

Nero did not go unpunished for this crime and others he committed, for he put an end to his life with his own hand. Here we may add a brief notice of some of these crimes.

We read in a certain history, admittedly apocryphal, that when Seneca, Nero's tutor, was looking forward to a reward worthy of his labors, Nero ordered him to choose which branch of a given tree he would prefer to be hanged from, saying that this was the reward he was going to receive. When Seneca asked why he was being condemned to death, Nero brandished a sharp sword over his head, and Seneca bowed his head and backed away from the sword, stricken with fear at the threat of death. Nero asked him: "Master, why do you

---

1 *Pope Leo and Marcellus* Fourth- and fifth-century popes, whose attestations are probably taken from the *Liber pontificalis*, a compilation of papal lives maintained throughout the Middle Ages.

bow your head and dodge the sword?" Seneca answered: "Because I am a man and therefore I fear death and am unwilling to die." Nero: "And I fear you even now, as I feared you as a child! That is why I cannot live in peace and quiet as long as you are alive!" "If I must die," said Seneca, "at least allow me to choose the mode of death that I would prefer!" Nero: "Choose quickly! Don't delay your death!" Then Seneca lay in a bathtub filled with water and opened the veins in both arms; and as the blood flowed out, his life ended. So his very name, Seneca, was a presage. *Se necans* means killing oneself, and though he was forced to do so, he died by his own hand.

[...]

The same apocryphal history tells us that Nero, obsessed by an evil madness, ordered his mother killed and cut open so that he could see how it had been for him in her womb.

[...]

Then Nero began to wonder about the manner and extent of the burning of Troy, and made Rome burn for seven days and seven nights. He watched the fire from the highest available tower, being delighted with the beauty of the flames and reciting verses from the *Iliad* in a grandiose, bombastic style.

The chronicles tell us that Nero fished with gold nets, and that he worked hard at music and singing so as to surpass all harpists and actors. He took a man as his wife and was accepted as wife by a man, Orosius[1] says. Finally the Romans could tolerate his insanity no longer, so they rose up against him and drove him out of the city. Seeing that no escape was possible, he sharpened a stick to a point with his teeth and drove it through his middle, thus putting an end to his life.[2] Elsewhere we read that he was devoured by wolves.

---

1 *Orosius* Paulus Orosius (385-?420 CE), Christian historian most famous for his *Historiarum adversum paganos* (*History Against the Pagans*).
2 *Finally the Romans ... his life.* Cf. *Siege* lines 903–20.

D. Other Medieval Anti-Semitisms and the Crusade Context

By the time *The Siege of Jerusalem* was written, Jews had not legally resided in England for about a century. King Edward I expelled Jews from England in 1290, and most English people of the late fourteenth century therefore had little to no experience of Jewish people or Judaism. The *idea* of the Jew, however, was persistent in many forms of narrative before and after the expulsion: in Christian biblical literature of course, but also in historical, legal, devotional, and popular literature. Such texts frequently cast Jews as moral, economic, or religious threats and included stock Jewish characters, scenes, and faults, including imputed responsibility for Jesus' death, attachments to money or deceptive behavior, the continuous torture of Christ or Christ figures, and the murder of children.

The idea of a Christian Holy Land also had special currency in the Middle Ages, an era punctuated by papally sponsored crusades to the East. As historian Jonathan Riley-Smith has put it, "The crusades dominated the thoughts and feelings of western Europeans between 1095 and 1500 so profoundly that there was scarcely a writer on contemporary affairs who did not at some point refer to one of them or to the fate of the settlements established in their wake."[1] The First Crusade climaxed in the siege and capture of Jerusalem in 1099, and, though Jerusalem was under Fatimid (Muslim) control at the time, echoes of biblical-prophetic narratives and historical resonances with the first-century destruction of Jerusalem were not lost on crusaders, nor on medieval chroniclers and poets. The western literary imagination of the first-century siege was deeply influenced by the late-eleventh-century crusade victory and by subsequent crusader attempts to maintain control of Jerusalem, as it also was by historical memory and accounts of crusader violence against non-Christians at home and abroad.

Though *The Siege of Jerusalem* was written in English in the late fourteenth century, and though its setting is primarily the first-century Roman Empire, medieval England's (anti-)Jewish history and crusad-

---

1   *What Were the Crusades?* 3rd ed. (San Francisco: Ignatius, 2002), 1.

ing history provide significant background and contexts for the poem. The passages below, arranged by genre and roughly chronologically, provide a sample of texts related to crusader interactions with Jews and Jerusalem (with a focus on the First Crusade conquest of Jerusalem and anti-Semitic riots in England preceding the Third Crusade), along with other pseudo-historical, legal, and literary representations of Jews that existed by or around the time the *Siege* poet was writing. Some Jewish responses are included.

1. Crusade Violence in Historical Writings

a. from Albert of Aachen, *History of the Journey to Jerusalem*[1] (c. 1125–50)

Albert of Aachen's Latin *Historia Ierosolimitana* (*History of the Journey to Jerusalem*) records the history of the First Crusade and the establishment of the crusader kingdom of Jerusalem to 1121 CE. Albert compiled his chronicle from eyewitness accounts and other sources, many of which are now lost. The following excerpt records events that occurred in 1096, at the beginning of the crusade, when thousands of Rhineland Jews were killed by crusaders on their way to Jerusalem. Many were forced to convert to Christianity; some chose suicide in the face of atrocities. Albert's account of these massacres, in his view associated with the so-called "People's Crusade," is the most detailed contemporary Christian account.

[A] large and innumerable host of Christians [assembled] from diverse kingdoms and lands; namely, from the realms of France, England, Flanders, and Lorraine.... I know not whether by a judgment of the Lord, or by some error of mind, they rose in a spirit of cruelty against the Jewish people scattered throughout these cities and slaughtered them without mercy, especially in the Kingdom of Lorraine, asserting it to be the beginning of their expedition and their duty against the enemies of the Christian faith. This slaughter of Jews was done first by citizens of Cologne. These suddenly fell upon a small band of Jews and severely wounded and killed many; they destroyed the

---

1 *History of the Journey to Jerusalem* English text from August Charles Krey, ed. and trans., *The First Crusade: The Accounts of Eyewitnesses and Participants* (Princeton: Princeton UP, 1921), 54–56.

houses and synagogues of the Jews and divided among themselves a very large amount of money. When the Jews saw this cruelty, about two hundred in the silence of the night began flight by boat to Neuss. The pilgrims and crusaders discovered them, and after taking away all their possessions, inflicted on them similar slaughter, leaving not even one alive.

Not long after this, they started upon their journey, as they had vowed, and arrived in a great multitude at the city of Mainz. There Count Emico, a nobleman, a very mighty man in this region, was awaiting, with a large band of Teutons, the arrival of the pilgrims who were coming thither from diverse lands by the King's highway.

The Jews of this city, knowing of the slaughter of their brethren, and that they themselves could not escape the hands of so many, fled in hope of safety to Bishop Rothard.[1] They put an infinite treasure in his guard and trust, having much faith in his protection, because he was Bishop of the city. Then that excellent Bishop of the city cautiously set aside the incredible amount of money received from them. He placed the Jews in the very spacious hall of his own house, away from the sight of Count Emico and his followers, that they might remain safe and sound in a very secure and strong place.

But Emico and the rest of his band held a council and, after sunrise, attacked the Jews in the hall with arrows and lances. Breaking the bolts and doors, they killed the Jews, about seven hundred in number, who in vain resisted the force and attack of so many thousands. They killed the women, also, and with their swords pierced tender children of whatever age and sex. The Jews, seeing that their Christian enemies were attacking them and their children, and that they were sparing no age, likewise fell upon one another, brother, children, wives, and sisters, and thus they perished at each other's hands. Horrible to say, mothers cut the throats of nursing children with knives and stabbed others, preferring them to perish thus by their own hands rather than to be killed by the weapons of the uncircumcised.[2]

From this cruel slaughter of the Jews a few escaped; and a few because of fear, rather than because of love of the Christian faith, were baptized. With very great spoils taken from these people, Count

---

1   *Bishop Rothard*   Ruthard, Archbishop of Mainz, 1089–1109 CE.
2   *the uncircumcised*   An epithet for Christians.

Emico … and all that intolerable company of men and women then continued on their way to Jerusalem, directing their course towards the Kingdom of Hungary, where passage along the royal highway was usually not denied the pilgrims. But on arriving at Wieselburg, the fortress of the King, which the rivers Danube and Leytha protect with marshes, the bridge and gate of the fortress were found closed by command of the King of Hungary,[1] for great fear had entered all the Hungarians because of the slaughter which had happened to their brethren.…

But while almost everything had turned out favorably for the Christians, and while they had penetrated the walls with great openings, by some chance or misfortune, I know not what, such great fear entered the whole army that they turned in flight, just as sheep are scattered and alarmed when wolves rush upon them. And seeking a refuge here and there, they forgot their companions.

Emico and some of his followers continued in their flight along the way by which they had come … [Some] escaped in flight toward Carinthia and Italy. So the hand of the Lord is believed to have been against the pilgrims, who had sinned by excessive impurity and fornication, and who had slaughtered the exiled Jews through greed of money, rather than for the sake of God's justice, although the Jews were opposed to Christ. The Lord is a just judge and orders no one unwillingly, or under compulsion, to come under the yoke of the Catholic faith.

b. from Eliezar bar Nathan, *Persecutions of 1096*[2] (c. 1150)

> One of three surviving Hebrew chronicles of the First Crusade, all of which are known by the title *Gezerot Tatnu* (*Persecutions of 1096*), Eliezar bar Nathan's text is an emotional lament for the Jewish communities of Speyer, Worms, Mainz, and Cologne—all decimated by crusading armies en route to Jerusalem—and the excerpt below can be read alongside Albert of Aachen's account of the Rhineland massacres. Eliezar himself lived in Mainz, and may have lived in Cologne at one

---

1 *King of Hungary* Kolomon I, who ruled 1095–1116 CE.
2 *Persecutions of 1096* English text from Shlomo Eidelberg, ed. and trans., *The Jews and the Crusaders: The Hebrew Chronicles of the First and Second Crusades* (Hoboken: KTAV, 1996), 79–80 and 83–85.

time. He was a prolific writer, particularly of liturgical poetry, some of which is incorporated here.

There arose arrogant people, a people of strange speech, a nation bitter and impetuous, Frenchmen and Germans, from all directions. They decided to set out for the Holy City,[1] there to seek their house of idolatry, banish the Ishmaelites,[2] and conquer the land for themselves. They decorated themselves prominently with their signs, by marking themselves upon their garments with their sign—a horizontal line over a vertical one—every man and woman whose heart yearned to go there,[3] until their ranks swelled so that the number of men, women, and children exceeded a locust horde; of them it was said: "The locusts have no king [yet go they forth all of them by bands]."[4]

Now it came to pass that as they passed through the towns where Jews dwelled, they said to themselves: "Look now, we are going to seek out our profanity and to take vengeance on the Ishmaelites for our messiah, when here are the Jews who murdered and crucified him. Let us first avenge ourselves on them and exterminate them from among the nations so that the name of Israel will no longer be remembered, or let them adopt our faith and acknowledge the offspring of promiscuity."[5]

When the Jewish communities learned of this, they were overcome by fear, trembling, and pains, as of a woman in travail. They resorted to the custom of their ancestors: prayer, charity, and repentance. They decreed fast days, scattered days as well as consecutive ones, fasting for three consecutive days, night and day. They cried to the Lord in their trouble, but He obstructed their prayer, concealing Himself in a cloud through which their prayers could not pass.[6] For it had been

---

1   *Holy City*   Jerusalem.
2   *Ishmaelites*   Those descended from Ishmael. In traditional Jewish exegesis, Ishmael is the ancestor of Arab peoples (Eliezar means to refer specifically to Muslims), distinct from the Jewish descendants of Isaac. See Genesis 17.18–21 and 21.8–21.
3   *They decorated ... go there*   Eliezar refers to the customary "sign of the cross" sewn onto the clothing of crusaders to signify their vow to go to Jerusalem.
4   *The locusts ... by bands*   Proverbs 30.27.
5   *offspring of promiscuity*   A pejorative epithet for Jesus that denies his mother's miraculous virginity.
6   *He obstructed ... could not pass*   Cf. Lamentations 3.44.

decreed by Him to take place "in the day when I visit,"[1] and this was the generation that had been chosen by Him to be His portion, for they had the strength and the fortitude to stand in His Sanctuary, and fulfill His word, and sanctify His Great Name[2] in His world. It is of such as these that King David said: "Bless the Lord, ye angels of His, ye mighty in strength, that fulfill His word."[3]

[...]

The enemy arose against them,[4] killing little children and women, youth and old men, viciously—all on one day—a nation of fierce countenance that does not respect the old nor show favor to the young.[5] The enemy showed no mercy for babes and sucklings, no pity for women about to give birth. They left no survivor or remnant but a dried date, and two or three pits, for all of them had been eager to sanctify the Name of Heaven. And when the enemy was upon them, they all cried out in a great voice, with one heart and one tongue: "Hear, O Israel," etc.[6]

Some of the pious old men wrapped themselves in their fringed prayer shawls and sat in the bishop's courtyard. They hastened to fulfill the will of their Creator, not wishing to flee just to be saved for temporal life, for lovingly they accepted Heaven's judgment. The foe hurled stones and arrows at them, but they did not scurry to flee. Women, too, girded their loins with strength[7] and slew their own sons and daughters, and then themselves. Tenderhearted men also mustered their strength and slaughtered their wives, sons, daughters, and infants. The most gentle and tender of women slaughtered the child of her delight.

---

1   *"in the day when I visit"*   Cf. Exodus 32.34 and Amos 3.14.

2   *sanctify His Great Name*   Refers to acts of martyrdom and self-sacrifice, where Jewish piety reflects back on god, called in Hebrew *kiddush ha-shem* (Sanctifying the Name).

3   *"Bless the Lord ... His word"*   Psalm 103.20.

4   *them*   The Jewish community at Mainz.

5   *a nation ... the young*   Deuteronomy 28.50.

6   *"Hear, O Israel," etc.*   Continues "the Lord Our God, the Lord is One." This prayer, known as the *Shema* (for its first Hebrew word), functions as a creed in Judaism. See Deuteronomy 6.4.

7   *Women ... with strength*   See Proverbs 31.17, where this verse is part of a poem in praise of the ideal woman.

Let the ears hearing this and its like be seared, for who has heard or seen the likes of it? Did it ever occur that there were one thousand *'Akedot'*[1] on a single day? The earth trembled over just one offering that occurred on the myrrh mountain.[2] Behold, the valiant ones cry without; the angels of peace weep bitterly.[3] But the heavens did not darken and the stars did not withhold their radiance! Why did not the sun and the moon turn dark, when one thousand three hundred holy souls were slain on a single day—among them babes and sucklings who had not sinned or transgressed—the souls of innocent poor people? Wilt Thou restrain Thyself for these things, O Lord?[4]

Sixty people were rescued on that day in the courtyard of the bishop. He took them to the villages of the Rheingau[5] in order to save them. There, too, the enemy assembled against them and slew them all. For because of our sins, the slayer had been given permission to injure. Wherever a Jew would flee to save his soul—there the rock would cry out from the wall.[6]

Two pious men were spared on that day because the enemy had defiled them[7] against their will. The name of one was Master Uri, and the name of the second was Master Isaac—the latter being accompanied by his two daughters. They, too, greatly sanctified the Name and now accepted upon themselves a death so awesome that it is not recorded in all Biblical admonitions. For on the eve of Pentecost,[8] Isaac, the son of David, the *Parnass,*[9] slaughtered his two daughters and set his house afire. Thereupon he and Master Uri went to the synagogue before the Holy Ark, and they both died there before the Lord, wholeheartedly yielding to the consuming flames. And it is of

---

1 *'Akedot'* Hebrew: bindings. Refers to Abraham's binding of Isaac (as a sacrifice) in Genesis 22.
2 *the myrhh mountain* The mountain where Abraham bound Isaac.
3 *Behold ... weep bitterly* Isaiah 33.7.
4 *Wilt thou ... O Lord?* Isaiah 64.12.
5 *of the Rheingau* Along the Rhine River.
6 *there the rock ... from the wall* Cf. Habakkuk 2.10–11.
7 *defiled them* Forced baptism on them.
8 *Pentecost* Not the Christian holiday but the Jewish holiday of Shavuot (50 days after Passover), in Jewish tradition the anniversary of the day Moses received the Torah on Mount Sinai.
9 *Parnass* A treasurer, in charge of community finances.

them and their like that it is written: "He who offers the sacrifice of thanksgiving honors Me."[1]

For the pious ones of Mainz I shall let out wailing like a jackal:

Woe is me for my calamity, severe is my wound, I declare:
"My tent has been pillaged and all my ropes have been broken: my children have left me."[2]

My heart goes out to the slain of Mainz, those valued as gold and as scarlet.
My heart ails for them while I must suppress my cries of woe,

Erudite as "the families of scribes that dwelt at Jabez: Tirathites, the Shimeathites, the Sucathites."[3] They were exterminated for my sins,
Being men that had wisdom and understanding to comprehend the Torah.

It is for them that I weep, that tears drop from my eye;
For the calamity of my people I am racked; darkness has descended, desolation has taken hold of me.

Elders have vanished from the gate; those who sound their voice to instruct me are no more.
This Torah—who will extol thee? Gone are those who were wont to utter your words in my ear!

Who will explain and teach me your esoteric knowledge and your curled locks?
At the inception of the night vigils, arise, and mourn before your Master!

For the life of those who were wont to utter your words, allow yourself no rest.
Strive my soul, battle for me, O Lord, defend my case and right my wrong!

---

1   "He who offers ... honors Me"   Psalm 50.23.
2   "My tent ... left me"   Cf. Jeremiah 10.20.
3   "the families ... Sucathites"   1 Chronicles 2.55.

Avenge me, avenge the blood of Your Saints, O Lord, my Master,
For naught can take their place. You have assured and told me—
I will avenge their blood which I have not avenged; and my dwell-
  ing is in Zion.[1]

As it is said: "And I will hold as innocent their blood which I have not
avenged; and the Lord dwelleth in Zion."[2] And it is said: "I have set
their blood upon the bare rock, that it should not be covered."[3]

The news reached Cologne on the fifth of the month, the eve of
Pentecost, and instilled mortal fear into the community. Everyone
fled to the houses of Gentile acquaintances and remained there.
On the following morning the enemies rose up and broke into the
houses, looting and plundering. The foe destroyed the synagogue and
removed the Torah Scrolls, desecrating them and casting them into
the streets to be trodden underfoot. On the very day that the Torah
was given, when the earth trembled and its pillars quivered, they now
tore, burned, and trod upon it—those wicked evildoers regarding
whom it is said: "Robbers have entered and profaned it."[4]

O God, will You not punish them for these acts? How long will
You look on at the wicked and remain silent? "See, O Lord, and be-
hold, how abject I am become."[5]

c. from Raymond d'Aguilers, *History of the Frankish Conquerors of
Jerusalem*[6] (c. 1100)

The *Historia francorum qui ceperint Ierusalem* (*History of the Frankish
Conquerors of Jerusalem*) is an eyewitness account of crusader travels
and victories up to the Battle of Ascalon (August 1099). It was written
in Latin very shortly after the events it records. Its author, Raymond
d'Aguilers, a priest from the Auvergne region of France, was part of
a group of Provençal crusaders, and he became chaplain to Count

---

1   *my dwelling is in Zion*   The end of the *kinah*, or poetic (liturgical) lamentation. In the
    original Hebrew, the letters that begin each line form an acrostic of the author's name.
2   *"And I will hold ... in Zion"* Joel 3.21.
3   *"I have set ... covered"* Ezekiel 24.8.
4   *"Robbers ... profaned it"* Ezekiel 7.22.
5   *"See, O Lord ... become"* Lamentations 1.11.
6   *History of the Frankish Conquerors of Jerusalem*   English text from Krey, ed. and trans., *The
    First Crusade*, 257–61.

Raymond IV of Toulouse, a leader of the French forces in the First Crusade. The excerpt below includes his description of the final assault and capture of Jerusalem in June-July 1099.

The Duke and the Counts of Normandy and Flanders placed Gaston of Beert in charge of the workmen who constructed machines. They built mantlets[1] and towers with which to attack the wall. The direction of this work was assigned to Gaston by the princes because he was a most noble lord, respected by all for his skill and reputation. He very cleverly hastened matters by dividing the work. The princes busied themselves with obtaining and bringing the material, while Gaston supervised the work of construction. Likewise, Count Raymond made William Ricau superintendent of the work on Mount Zion[2] and placed the Bishop of Albara[3] in charge of the Saracens[4] and others who brought in the timber. The Count's men had taken many Saracen castles and villages and forced the Saracens to work, as though they were their serfs. Thus for the construction of machines at Jerusalem fifty or sixty men carried on their shoulders a great beam that could not have been dragged by four pair of oxen. What more shall I say? All worked with a singleness of purpose, no one was slothful, and no hands were idle. All worked without wages, except the artisans, who were paid from a collection taken from the people. However, Count Raymond paid his workmen from his own treasury. Surely the hand of the Lord was with us and aided those who were working!

When our efforts were ended and the machines completed, the princes held a council and announced: "Let all prepare themselves for a battle on Thursday; in the meantime, let us pray, fast, and give alms. Hand over your animals and your boys to the artisans and carpenters, that they may bring in beams, poles, stakes, and branches to make mantlets. Two knights should make one mantlet and one scaling lad-

---

1 *mantlets* Large portable shelters or walls, used to protect advancing forces from projectiles.
2 *Mount Zion* Just outside the city walls, to the south.
3 *Albara* Bara, Syria was conquered by crusaders in 1098.
4 *Saracens* Medieval term for eastern non-Christians, applied to people of Arab descent or Muslims, though its meaning is variable. Raymond uses it to describe residents of conquered cities, who are being used as servants, and to describe the defenders of Jerusalem, a group that would have included Muslims and Jews (eastern Christians had been expelled from the city by this time).

der. Do not hesitate to work for the Lord, for your labors will soon be ended." This was willingly done by all. Then it was decided what part of the city each leader should attack and where his machines should be located.

Meanwhile, the Saracens in the city, noting the great number of machines that we had constructed, strengthened the weaker parts of the wall, so that it seemed that they could be taken only by the most desperate efforts. Because the Saracens had made so many and such strong fortifications to oppose our machines, the Duke, the Count of Flanders, and the Count of Normandy spent the night before the day set for the attack moving their machines, mantlets, and platforms to that side of the city which is between the church of St. Stephen and the valley of Josaphat.[1] You who read this must not think that this was a light undertaking, for the machines were carried in parts almost a mile to the place where they were to be set up. When morning came and the Saracens saw that all the machinery and tents had been moved during the night, they were amazed. Not only the Saracens were astonished, but our people as well, for they recognized that the hand of the Lord was with us. The change was made because the new point chosen for attack was more level, and thus suitable for moving the machines up to the walls, which cannot be done unless the ground is level; and also because that part of the city seemed to be weaker, having remained unfortified, as it was some distance from our camp. This part of the city is on the north.

Count Raymond and his men worked equally hard on Mount Zion, but they had much assistance from William Embraico[2] and the Genoese sailors, who, although they had lost their ships at Joppa,[3] as we have already related, had been able, nevertheless, to save ropes, mallets, spikes, axes, and hatchets, which were very necessary to us. But why delay the story? The appointed day arrived and the attack began. However, I want to say this first, that, according to our estimate and that of many others, there were sixty thousand fighting men within the city, not counting the women and those unable to bear

---

1 *valley of Josaphat* Traditionally associated with the Cedron valley.

2 *William Embraico* Guglielmo Embriaco, a Genoese merchant and naval leader, who helped crusaders capture the city of Jaffa and dismantled his damaged ships to provide material for siege engines.

3 *Joppa* Jaffa.

arms, and there were not many of these. At the most we did not have more than twelve thousand able to bear arms, for there were many poor people and many sick. There were twelve or thirteen hundred knights in our army, as I reckon it, not more. I say this that you may realize that nothing, whether great or small, which is undertaken in the name of the Lord can fail, as the following pages show.

Our men began to undermine the towers and walls. From every side stones were hurled from the *tormenti* and the *petrariae*,[1] and so many arrows that they fell like hail. The servants of God bore this patiently, sustained by the premises of their faith, whether they should be killed or should presently prevail over their enemies. The battle showed no indication of victory, but when the machines were drawn nearer to the walls, they hurled not only stones and arrows, but also burning wood and straw. The wood was dipped in pitch, wax, and sulphur; then straw and tow were fastened on by an iron band, and, when lighted, these firebrands were shot from the machines. They were all bound together by an iron band, I say, so that wherever they fell, the whole mass held together and continued to burn. Such missiles, burning as they shot upward, could not be resisted by swords or by high walls; it was not even possible for the defenders to find safety down behind the walls. Thus the fight continued from the rising to the setting sun in such splendid fashion that it is difficult to believe anything more glorious was ever done. Then we called on Almighty God, our Leader and Guide, confident in His mercy. Night brought fear to both sides. The Saracens feared that we would take the city during the night or on the next day, for the outer works were broken through and the ditch was filled, so that it was possible to make an entrance through the wall very quickly. On our part, we feared only that the Saracens would set fire to the machines that were moved close to the walls, and thus improve their situation. So on both sides it was a night of watchfulness, labor, and sleepless caution: on one side, most certain hope, on the other doubtful fear. We gladly labored to capture the city for the glory of God, they less willingly strove to resist our efforts for the sake of the laws of Mohammed. It is hard to believe how great were the efforts made on both sides during the night.

---

1   *the tormenti and the petrariae*   Latin: siege machines that hurl projectiles.

When the morning came, our men eagerly rushed to the walls and dragged the machines forward, but the Saracens had constructed so many machines that for each one of ours they now had nine or ten. Thus they greatly interfered with our efforts. This was the ninth day, on which the priest had said that we would capture the city.[1] But why do I delay so long? Our machines were now shaken apart by the blows of many stones, and our men lagged because they were very weary. However, there remained the mercy of the Lord which is never overcome nor conquered, but is always a source of support in times of adversity. One incident must not be omitted. Two women tried to bewitch one of the hurling machines, but a stone struck and crushed them, as well as three slaves, so that their lives were extinguished and the evil incantations averted.

By noon our men were greatly discouraged. They were weary and at the end of their resources. There were still many of the enemy opposing each one of our men; the walls were very high and strong, and the great resources and skill that the enemy exhibited in repairing their defenses seemed too great for us to overcome. But, while we hesitated, irresolute, and the enemy exulted in our discomfiture, the healing mercy of God inspired us and turned our sorrow into joy, for the Lord did not forsake us. While a council was being held to decide whether or not our machines should be withdrawn, for some were burned and the rest badly shaken to pieces, a knight on the Mount of Olives[2] began to wave his shield to those who were with the Count and others, signaling them to advance. Who this knight was we have been unable to find out. At this signal our men began to take heart, and some began to batter down the wall, while others began to ascend by means of scaling ladders and ropes. Our archers shot burning fire-brands, and in this way checked the attack that the Saracens were making upon the wooden towers of the Duke and the two Counts. These firebrands, moreover, were wrapped in cotton. This shower of fire drove the defenders from the walls. Then the Count quickly released the long drawbridge which had protected the side of the wooden tower next to the wall, and it swung down from the top, being fastened to the middle of the tower, making a bridge over which

---

1   *the priest ... capture the city*   Refers to a reported vision of Bishop Ademar of Le Puy, a papal legate who accompanied Count Raymond's forces but died before the siege of Jerusalem.
2   *Mount of Olives*   Just outside the city walls, to the east.

the men began to enter Jerusalem bravely and fearlessly. Among those who entered first were Tancred and the Duke of Lorraine,[1] and the amount of blood that they shed on that day is incredible. All ascended after them, and the Saracens now began to suffer.

Strange to relate, however, at this very time when the city was practically captured by the Franks, the Saracens were still fighting on the other side, where the Count was attacking the wall as though the city should never be captured. But now that our men had possession of the walls and towers, wonderful sights were to be seen. Some of our men (and this was more merciful) cut off the heads of their enemies; others shot them with arrows, so that they fell from the towers; others tortured them longer by casting them into the flames. Piles of heads, hands, and feet were to be seen in the streets of the city. It was necessary to pick one's way over the bodies of men and horses. But these were small matters compared to what happened at the Temple of Solomon, a place where religious services are ordinarily chanted. What happened there? If I tell the truth, it will exceed your powers of belief. So let it suffice to say this much, at least, that in the Temple and porch of Solomon, men rode in blood up to their knees and bridle reins. Indeed, it was a just and splendid judgment of God that this place should be filled with the blood of the unbelievers, since it had suffered so long from their blasphemies. The city was filled with corpses and blood. Some of the enemy took refuge in the Tower of David, and, petitioning Count Raymond for protection, surrendered the Tower into his hands.

Now that the city was taken, it was well worth all our previous labors and hardships to see the devotion of the pilgrims at the Holy Sepulchre. How they rejoiced and exulted and sang a new song to the Lord! For their hearts offered prayers of praise to God, victorious and triumphant, which cannot be told in words. A new day, new joy, new and perpetual gladness, the consummation of our labor and devotion, drew forth from all new words and new songs. This day, I say, will be famous in all future ages, for it turned our labors and sorrows into joy and exultation; this day, I say, marks the justification of all Christianity, the humiliation of paganism, and the renewal of our faith. "This

---

1 *Tancred and the Duke of Lorraine* Tancred, a military leader from the Norman contingent, and Godfrey of Bouillon, Duke of Lower Lorraine 1087–1100 CE.

is the day which the Lord hath made, let us rejoice and be glad in it,"[1] for on this day the Lord revealed Himself to His people and blessed them.

d. from William of Newburgh, *The History of English Affairs*[2] (c. 1198)

> The *Historia de rebus anglicis* (*History of English Affairs*) is a Latin chronicle of England from the Norman Conquest in 1066 to 1198, written by an Augustinian canon named William, from Newburgh Priory in North Yorkshire. The excerpt here includes William's critical account of riots in which many of the York Jewish community were massacred, or killed themselves, while besieged in a castle keep at the site now known as Clifford's Tower. The York massacre took place 16–17 March 1190 (a Friday and Saturday, the Sabbath before Passover), following anti-Jewish violence that began in September 1189 around King Richard I's coronation ceremony in London. Richard I (also known as Richard the Lionheart) was a leader of the Third Crusade and had vowed to go to the Holy Land in 1187, in response to the loss of Jerusalem to Saladin. The English were heavily taxed to support his expedition. As William makes clear below, the religious, economic, and political motivations of English crusaders were difficult to untangle.

The zeal of the Christians against the Jews in England ... broke out fiercely. It was not indeed sincere, that is, solely for the sake of the faith, but in rivalry for the luck of others or from envy of their good fortune. Bold and greedy men thought that they were doing an act pleasing to God, while they robbed or destroyed rebels against Christ and carried out the work of their own cupidity with savage joy and without any, or only the slightest, scruple of conscience—God's justice, indeed, by no means approving such deeds but cunningly ordaining that in this way the insolence of that perfidious people might be checked and their blaspheming tongues curbed....

---

1 *"This is the day ... glad in it"* Psalm 118.24.
2 *The History of English Affairs* English text from Jacob Rader Marcus, ed. and trans., *The Jew in the Medieval World: A Source Book: 315–1791*. Rev. ed. by Marc Saperstein (Cincinnati: Hebrew Union College Press, 1999), 147–51.

The men of York were restrained neither by fear of the hot-tempered King nor the vigor of the laws, nor by feelings of humanity, from satiating their fury with the total ruin of their perfidious fellow-citizens and from rooting out the whole race in their city. And as this was a very remarkable occurrence, it ought to be transmitted to posterity at greater length....

When the King had established himself across the sea, many of the province of York plotted against the Jews, not being able to suffer their opulence, when they themselves were in need, and, without any scruple of Christian conscience, thirsting for the blood of infidels from greed for booty. The leaders of this daring plan were some of the nobles indebted to the impious usurers in large sums. Some of these, having given up their estates to them for the money they had received, were now oppressed by great want; some, bound by their own sureties, were pressed by the exactions of the Treasury to satisfy the royal usurers.

Some, too, of those who had taken the cross[1] and were on the point of starting for Jerusalem, were more easily induced to defray the expenses of the journey undertaken for the Lord's sake out of the booty taken from the Lord's enemies, especially as they had little fear of being questioned for the deed when they had started on their journey.

One stormy night no small part of the city became on fire either by chance or, as is believed, by arson perpetrated by the conspirators, so that the citizens were occupied with their own houses in fear of the fire spreading. There was nothing, therefore, in the way of the robbers, and an armed band of the conspirators, with great violence and tools prepared for the purpose, burst into the house of the before-mentioned Benedict,[2] who had miserably died at London as was mentioned above. There his widow and children with many others dwelt; all of those who were in it were slain and the roof put on fire.

And while the fire gloomily increased in strength, the robbers seized their booty and left the burning house, and by help of the darkness retired unobserved and heavy laden. The Jews, and especially

---

1 *taken the cross* Vowed to go on crusade.
2 *Benedict* A prominent York Jew who attended Richard I's coronation and died in the aftermath of the associated London riots.

their leader Joce,[1] in consternation at this misdeed, having begged the assistance of the Warden of the royal castle, carried into it huge weights of their monies equal to royal treasures, and took more vigilant guard of the rest at their houses.

But after a few days these nocturnal thieves returned with greater confidence and boldness and many joined them; they boldly besieged Joce's house which rivalled a noble citadel in the scale and stoutness of its construction. At length they captured and pillaged it, and then set it on fire after having removed by sword or fire all those whom an unlucky chance had kept in it. For Joce a little before had wisely anticipated this mischance and had removed with his wife and children into the castle, and the rest of the Jews did the same, only a few remaining outside as victims.

When the robbers had departed with so great a reward of their daring, a promiscuous mob rushed up at break of day and tore to pieces the furniture which remained from the spoilers and the fire. Then at length those who had personally held the Jews in hatred, no longer having any fear of public rigor, began to rage against them openly and with abundant license. No longer content with their substance, they gave to all found outside the castle the option of sacred baptism or the extreme penalty. Thereupon some were baptized and feignedly joined Christianity to escape death. But those who refused to accept the sacrament of life, even as a matter of pretense, were butchered without mercy.

While all this was happening the multitude who had escaped into the castle seemed to be in safety. But the Warden of the castle, having gone out on some business, when he wished to return was not readmitted by the trembling multitude, uncertain in whom to trust and fearing that perchance his fidelity to them was tottering, and that being bribed he was about to give up to their enemies those whom he should protect. But he immediately went to the sheriff of the county who happened to be at York with a large body of the county soldiers, and complained to him that the Jews had cheated him out of the castle entrusted to him. The sheriff became indignant and raged against the Jews. The leaders of the conspiracy fanned his fury, alleging that the timid precaution of those poor wretches was an

---

1 *Joce* Josce of York, a financier and community leader.

insolent seizure of the royal castle and would cause injury to our lord, the King. And when many declared that such traitors were to be got at by some means or another, and the royal castle taken out of their hands, the sheriff ordered the people to be summoned and the castle to be besieged.

The irrevocable word went forth, the zeal of the Christian folk was inflamed, immense masses of armed men both from the town and the country were clustered round the citadel. Then the sheriff, struck with regret at his order, tried in vain to recall it and wished to prohibit the siege of the castle. But he could by no influence of reason or authority keep back their inflamed minds from carrying out what they had begun. It is true the nobles of the city and the more weighty citizens, fearing the danger of a royal movement, cautiously declined such a great transgression. But the whole of the work-people and all the youth of the town and a large number of the country folk, together with soldiers not a few, came with such alacrity and joined in the cruel business as if each man was seeking his own gain. And there were not lacking many clergymen, among whom a certain hermit seemed more vehement than the rest....

Accordingly the Jews were besieged in the royal tower, and the besieged lacked a sufficient supply of provisions, and would have been quickly starved out by hunger even if no one attacked them from without. But they did not have either a sufficient stock of arms for their own safety or for repelling the enemy. Naturally they held back the threatening enemy with stones taken from the inner wall. The tower was stoutly besieged for several days, and at length the machines which had been prepared for the purpose were brought into position....

When the machines were thus moved into position, the taking of the tower became certain, and it was no longer doubtful that the fatal hour was nearing for the besieged. On the following night the besiegers were quiet, rejoicing in the certainty of their approaching victory. But the Jews were brave, and braced up by their very despair, had little rest, discussing what they should do in such an extremity.... [At the advice of their rabbi, the noted Yomtob of Joigny, many killed themselves, after first setting fire to the tower. Those who were left offered to convert, but were mercilessly slaughtered by the aroused mob.]

The look of things in the city was at that time horrid and nauseous, and round the citadel were lying scattered the corpses of so many unfortunates still unburied. But when the slaughter was over, the conspirators immediately went to the Cathedral and caused the terrified guardians, with violent threats, to hand over the records of the debts placed there by which the Christians were oppressed by the royal Jewish usurers. Thereupon they destroyed these records of profane avarice in the middle of the church with the sacred fires to release both themselves and many others. Which being done, those of the conspirators who had taken the cross went on their proposed journey before any inquest; but the rest remained in the country in fear of an inquiry. Such were the things that happened at York at the time of the Lord's Passion, that is, the day before Palm Sunday.

e. from Ephraim of Bonn, "In England, 1189"[1] (c. 1196)

> Ephraim ben Jacob of Bonn, a prolific liturgical poet and historian, is best known as the author of the *Sefer Zekhirah* (*Book of Remembrance*), the only Hebrew account of the Second Crusade (1145–49 CE), during which Ephraim was an adolescent in Cologne. The excerpt below is from one of his lesser-known works, sometimes called the *Book of Historical Records*, a compilation of descriptions of Jewish persecutions that preceded the Third Crusade. The work records incidents that occurred between 1171 and 1196 across England, France, Germany, and Austria, and was probably written when Ephraim was in his 60s and serving as head of the rabbinic court at Bonn. Included here is Ephraim's description of the York massacre of 1190, which can be read alongside William of Newburgh's account of the same event.

In the year 4950[2] a disaster for Israel was ordained, because a king was made in the islands of the sea called England—and it happened on the day that he was made king and the king's crown was placed on his head, in the city of London. In the king's palace,[3] which is outside of

---

1   *"In England, 1189"*   English text copyright Shamma A. Boyarin © 2013, translated from the Hebrew as it appears in *Sefer Gezerot Ashkenaz ve-Zorfat*, ed. A.M. Habermann (Jerusalem: Tarshish, 1945), 127.
2   *the year 4950*   1189 CE. Ephraim uses the Jewish calendar.
3   *the king's palace*   Richard I was crowned 3 September 1189 in Westminster Abbey.

the city, a large group from England and France gathered. The Jews came as well, their leaders and wealthy among them, to bring a gift to the king. Some wicked men began to say, "It is not right that the Jews come to see the king's crown, with which priests and monks crown him on the day he is crowned as king!" And they pushed them and tormented them, and the king did not know. Then a rumor passed through the city, saying, "The king has commanded the destruction of the Jews!" They began to beat them and to destroy their houses and towers, and they killed thirty men among them. A few of them slaughtered themselves and their children. The distinguished rabbi, Rabbi Jacob of Orléans, died there for the sake of sanctifying the name. The king did not know any of this, because when he heard the sound of the mob in the city he asked, "What is this sound of commotion?" The gatekeeper said to him, "It is nothing, just the sound of the youth playing and rejoicing." And afterwards, when he found out the truth, he commanded that the gatekeeper be tied to the tails of horses, dragged and tossed throughout the streets and markets until his spirit departed. And he died a bad death. Blessed is the God who gives vengeance.

Afterwards in the year 4951,[1] the misguided arose against the people of God in the city of Evorich,[2] which is in England, on the day of the Great Sabbath,[3] and so the time of the miracle[4] turned into violence and punishment. They escaped to the house of prayer, for they thought it would be a place of refuge.[5] Then Rabbi Yom Tov stood up, and he slaughtered about sixty souls. Others slaughtered as well. And there was one who commanded his one and only son be slaughtered, so tender and delicate that he would never venture to set foot on the ground.[6]

There are those of them who were burned for the sake of the unity of their creator. The number of those killed and burned was about

---

1   *the year 4951*   1190 CE.

2   *Evorich*   A Hebraicized form of the Latin name for the city of York, Eboracum.

3   *Great Sabbath*   Shabbat Ha-Gadol, the sabbath before Passover.

4   *miracle*   I.e., the exodus of Israel from Egypt, which Passover commemorates.

5   *They escaped … place of refuge*   In Ephraim's version of the story, the Jews of York take refuge in a synagogue rather than the castle keep.

6   *so tender … ground*   See Deuteronomy 28.46–57, where this verse (28.56) is part of a list of punishments that will befall Israel during a siege if Israelites are disobedient to God, including parents forced to kill or eat their children.

one hundred and fifty holy souls, and their houses were destroyed, and gold and silver was pillaged. And the choicest of the books—which they had written many of, more desirable than gold, than much fine gold,[1] of which there are none as worthy in attractiveness and beauty—were brought to Cologne and other places and sold to the Jews.

And thus did our enemies do in several towns, and there they slaughtered them[2] and burned them. In one city, where there were only proselytes,[3] about twenty people—an assembly of converts is considered an assembly.[4] They killed them all. They did not want to be polluted by putrid water,[5] so they all sanctified the highest name.

2. Ritual Murder Libel: Selections from Thomas of Monmouth, *The Passion of William of Norwich*[6] (c. 1173)

Though the papacy consistently rejected the validity of such claims (see the Bull of Pope Gregory X below), medieval European Jews were repeatedly accused of murdering Christian boys in mockery or imitation of the killing of Christ. The first documented instance was recorded in Latin by Thomas of Monmouth, a Benedictine monk at Norwich in England. His *Passio Willelmi Norwicensis* (*The Passion of William of Norwich*) tells the story of the youth and martyr's death of a boy called William and documents miracles that followed. Completed by 1173, almost 30 years after William died in March 1144, Thomas's account of the case includes imagined secret events and conversations, conspiracy theories, embellished second-hand witness accounts, and the testimony of an otherwise unknown convert from Judaism named Theobald. The text is explicitly interested in establishing William's

---

1   *more desirable ... fine gold*   Psalm 19.10.

2   *them*   I.e., the Jews in those towns.

3   *proselytes*   Converts to Judaism.

4   *assembly*   Required community for liturgical purposes. The Talmud states in several places that an assembly of converts is not an assembly; Ephraim rejects this principle based on the example of this community.

5   *They did not ... putrid water*   I.e., the converts refused baptismal waters; they would not return to Christianity.

6   *The Passion of William of Norwich*   English text from A. Jessop and M.R. James, ed. and trans., *The Life and Miracles of St. William of Norwich* (Cambridge: Cambridge UP, 1896), 14–25 and 93–94.

sanctity, and it thus embraces biblical typology and is patterned on other saints' lives. The excerpt below includes Thomas's description of the murder itself, and his account of the convert Theobald's argument against the Norwich Jews.

[Book 1.] iii. How he [William] was wont to resort to the Jews, and having been chid by his own people for doing so, how he withdrew himself from them.

When therefore he was flourishing in this blessed boyhood of his, and had attained to his eighth year, he was entrusted to the skinners[1] to be taught their craft. Gifted with a teachable disposition and bringing industry to bear upon it, in a short time he far surpassed lads of his own age in the craft aforesaid, and he equalled some who had been his teachers. So leaving the country, drawn by a divine urge he betook himself to the city and lodged with a very famous master of that craft, and some time passed away. He was seldom in the country, but was occupied in the city and sedulously gave himself to the practice of his craft, and thus reached his twelfth year.

Now, while he was staying in Norwich, the Jews who were settled there and required their cloaks or their robes or other garments (whether pledged to them, or their own property) to be repaired, preferred him before all other skinners. For they esteemed him to be especially fit for their work, either because they had learnt that he was guileless and skillful, or, because attracted to him by their avarice, they thought they could bargain with him for a lower price. Or, as I rather believe, because by the ordering of divine Providence he had been predestined to martyrdom from the beginning of time, and gradually step by step was drawn on, and chosen to be made a mock of and to be put to death by the Jews, in scorn of the Lord's Passion, as one of little foresight, and so the more fit for them. For I have learnt from certain Jews, who were afterwards converted to the Christian faith, how that at that time they had planned to do this very thing with some Christian, and in order to carry out their malignant purpose, at the beginning of Lent they had made choice of the boy William, being twelve years of age and a boy of unusual innocence. So it came to pass that when the holy boy, ignorant of the treachery that

---

1 *skinners* Makers and merchants of leather products.

had been planned, had frequent dealings with the Jews, he was taken to task by Godwin the priest, who had the boy's aunt as his wife, and by a certain Wulward with whom he lodged, and he was prohibited from going in and out among them any more. But the Jews, annoyed at the thwarting of their designs, tried with all their might to patch up a new scheme of wickedness, and all the more vehemently as the day for carrying out the crime they had determined upon drew near, and the victim which they had thought they had already secured had slipped out of their wicked hands. Accordingly, collecting all the cunning of their crafty plots, they found—I am not sure whether he was a Christian or a Jew—a man who was a most treacherous fellow and just the fitting person for carrying out their execrable crime, and with all haste—for their Passover was coming on in three days—they sent him to find out and bring back with him the victim which, as I said before, had slipped out of their hands.

iv. How he was seduced by the Jews' messenger.

At the dawn of day, on the Monday after Palm Sunday,[1] that detestable messenger of the Jews set out to execute the business that was committed to him, and at last the boy William, after being searched for with very great care, was found. When he was found, he got round him with cunning wordy tricks, and so deceived him with his lying promises. For he pretended that he was the cook of William, Archdeacon of Norwich,[2] and that he wished to have him as a helper in the kitchen, where if he should continue steadily with him he would get many advantages in his situation. The simple boy was deceived, and trusted himself to the man; but, wishing to have his mother's favourable consent—for his father had died by this time—he started with the fellow to find her. When they had come to where she was, the boy told her the cause of his errand, and the traitor according to the tenour of his previous offer cast the net of his treachery. So that son of perdition by many promises easily prevailed upon the boy's mind by his tempting offers. Yet at first he could not at all gain the mother's consent; but when the scoundrel persisted the innocent boy agreed though his mother, moved by presentiment, resisted, and in

---

1   *Monday after Palm Sunday*   20 March 1144, also the first night of Passover in this year.
2   *William, Archdeacon of Norwich*   Who held the office 1124–50 CE.

her motherly affection feeling some fear for her son. On one side was the traitor, on the other the mother. He begs; she refuses. He begs, but only that he may make away with the boy. She refuses, afraid lest she should lose him. He asserts that he is the Archdeacon's cook, but she does not at all believe him. So between her and the other you might have seen a struggle as between a sheep and a wolf (who seemed at the first sight far the strongest) in defence of a third. The lamb was between them. Here stood the sheep and there the wolf. The wolf stands to it that he may rend and devour; the sheep holds her ground that she may rescue and save. But because the boy, being fascinated, favoured the one and kept on incessantly begging the consent of the other, the mother, partly overcome by her son's prayers and partly seduced by the man's fair promises, at last was compelled against her will to give way. She begged, however, for delay till after Easter; but the traitor swore he would not wait three days,[1] not for thirty pieces of silver.[2] The mother refused to let him go, and vowed she would not let him go before Easter. So the traitor took three shillings from his purse with intent to get the better of the mother's fancy and to bend the fickle stubbornness of a fickle woman, seduced by the glitter of money to the lust of gain. Thus the money was offered as the price of the innocent's service, or rather in truth as the price of his blood. But not even yet was the mother's devotion appeased, nor the presentiment of a coming evil easily removed. The wrangling still went on: on one side with prayers, and on the other with the pieces of silver, if so be that, though he could not prevail upon her stubbornness by his continual offers, the brightness of the coins that smiled at her might serve as a lure to her avarice. So the mother's mind was cruelly vanquished by these, even though the maternal affection only slowly gave way under the temptation and, seduced at last by the shining pieces of silver, she was the victim of her covetousness, and once overcome *nolens volens*[3] she became inclined to that which yet she was averse to. What need of many words? The mother being gained over, the lamb

---

1   *She begged ... three days*   The relative dates of Easter and Passover are negotiated here. William's mother begs delay until Easter Monday (27 March), which coincided with the end of Passover in 1144. The implication is that this timing matters to the Jews' intentions.
2   *thirty pieces of silver*   Cf. the betrayal of Jesus in Matthew 26.14–16. See also *Siege*, lines 1305–20.
3   *nolens volens*   Latin: unwilling (or) willing.

was handed over to the wolf, and the boy William was given up to the betrayer.

v. How on his going to the Jews he was taken, mocked and slain.

In the morning accordingly that traitor, the imitator in almost everything of the traitor Judas,[1] returns to Norwich with the boy, and as he was passing by the house of the boy's aunt he went in with him and said that the mother had entrusted the boy to himself, and then he went out again hastily. But the boy's aunt said quickly to her daughter, "Follow them at once, and take care you find out where that man is leading off the boy to." Thus the girl ran out to explore the way they were going; and she followed them at a distance as they turned about through some private alleys, and at last she saw them entering cautiously into the house of a certain Jew, and immediately she heard the door shut. When she saw this she went back to her mother and told her what she had seen.

Then the boy, like an innocent lamb, was led to the slaughter.[2] He was treated kindly by the Jews at first, and, ignorant of what was being prepared for him, he was kept till the morrow. But on the next day, which in that year was the Passover[3] for them, after the singing of the hymns appointed for the day in the synagogue, the chiefs of the Jews assembled in the house of the Jew aforesaid suddenly seized hold of the boy William as he was having his dinner and in no fear of any treachery, and ill-treated him in various horrible ways. For while some of them held him behind, others opened his mouth and introduced an instrument of torture which is called a teazle and, fixing it by straps through both jaws to the back of his neck, they fastened it with a knot as tightly as it could be drawn. After that, taking a short piece of rope of about the thickness of one's little finger and tying three knots in it at certain distances marked out, they bound round that innocent head with it from the forehead to the back, forcing the middle knot into his forehead and the two others into his temples, the two ends of the rope being most tightly stretched at the back of his head and fastened in a very tight knot. The ends of the rope were then passed round his neck and carried round his throat under his

---

1   *the traitor Judas* I.e., Judas Iscariot.
2   *lamb ... to the slaughter* Cf. Isaiah 53.7, Jeremiah 11.19, and Acts 8.32 (which cites Isaiah).
3   *on the next day ... Passover* 21 March 1144, a Tuesday.

chin, and there they finished off this dreadful engine of torture in a fifth knot.

But not even yet could the cruelty of the torturers be satisfied without adding even more severe pains. Having shaved his head, they stabbed it with countless thorn points,[1] and made the blood come horribly from the wounds they made. And so cruel were they and so eager to inflict pain that it was difficult to say whether they were more cruel or more ingenious in their tortures. For their skill in torturing kept up the strength of their cruelty and ministered arms thereto. And thus, while these enemies of the Christian name were rioting in the spirit of malignity around the boy, some of those present adjudged him to be fixed to a Cross in mockery of the Lord's Passion, as though they would say: "even as we condemned the Christ to a shameful death, so let us also condemn the Christian, so that, uniting the Lord and his servant in a like punishment, we may retort upon themselves the pain of that reproach which they impute to us."

Conspiring, therefore, to accomplish the crime of this great and detestable malice, they next laid their blood-stained hands upon the innocent victim, and having lifted him from the ground and fastened him upon the Cross, they vied with one another in their efforts to make an end of him. And we, after enquiring into the matter very diligently, did both find the house, and discovered some most certain marks in it of what had been done there. For the report goes that there was there instead of a cross a post set up between two other posts, and a beam stretched across the midmost post and attached to the other on either side. And as we afterwards discovered, from the marks of the wounds and of the bands, the right hand and foot had been tightly bound and fastened with cords, but the left hand and foot were pierced with two nails: so in fact the deed was done by design that, in case at any time he should be found, when the fastenings of the nails were discovered it might not be supposed that he had been killed by Jews rather than by Christians.[2] But while in

---

1 *countless thorn points* Thomas implies an imitation of the crown of thorns placed on the head of Jesus in Matthew 27.29, Mark 15.17–18, and John 19.2–5.

2 *so in fact … by Christians* Nails through both hands and both feet would make the wounds too obviously crucifixion-like and therefore implicate the Jews. Thomas argues that deviation from Christ's wounds takes suspicion off the Jewish community and therefore must be part of the Jews' plan.

doing these things they were adding pang to pang and wound to wound, and yet were not able to satisfy their heartless cruelty and their inborn hatred of the Christian name, lo! after all these many and great tortures, they inflicted a frightful wound in his left side,[1] reaching even to his inmost heart, and as though to make an end of all they extinguished his mortal life so far as it was in their power. And since many streams of blood were running down from all parts of his body, then, to stop the blood and to wash and close the wounds, they poured boiling water over him.

Thus then the glorious boy and martyr of Christ, William, dying the death of time in reproach of the Lord's death, but crowned with the blood of a glorious martyrdom, entered into the kingdom of glory on high to live for ever. Whose soul rejoiceth blissfully in heaven among the bright hosts of the saints, and whose body by the omnipotence of the divine mercy worketh miracles upon earth.

vi. How they took counsel about hiding him.

Thus, their wicked purpose having been carried out, the Jews consulting with one another about what else was to be done, taking down his lifeless body from the post, began to plot what they should do with it. Many proposed that it should be thrown into the draught-house[2] as if to increase the shame and disgrace; but some of the more crafty ones thought that it ought to be hidden in the ground, lest the Christians by some means or other should succeed in finding it. But the dispensation of the divine mercy, which provided that so illustrious a martyr should be made known to posterity, neither allowed him to be flung into an unclean place nor be hidden in the earth. Therefore by the divine purpose disposing the matter, it came to pass that while they were in doubt and quite uncertain what they should do, they all came to an agreement that till they could think the matter out more carefully they should keep him for awhile in some secret place. But the next day at dawn they came together again to settle the business; and—as we learnt afterwards from one of them—while they were discussing and still quite undecided what they should do, one of them who was of great authority among them—a divine impulse inspir-

---

1   *wound in his left side*   Another allusion to Christ's wounds. See John 19.34.
2   *draught-house*   Outdoor lavatory, latrine.

ing and impelling him—is reported to have given his advice thus: "Hearken unto me, brethren zealous for the divine law. I think it would be quite useless for us, and I fear it would be perilous hereafter, if this Christian's carcass were to be flung into our cesspool or buried in the ground on our premises. For since we are living in hired houses, if within a month or less we are forced for some reason to leave these premises and go elsewhere, I am very much afraid—and I shall be very much surprised if it does not turn out so—of what must follow upon our departure. For, as sure as we go, the Christians when they come in will certainly examine everything: and then who can believe that they will not, to shame us, clear out our cesspools, or, filling up the old sewers, dig new ones? And what then? The probability is that the body will be easily found, whether the sewers are cleaned out or new ones dug. And if the body be found the deed will surely not be attributed to Christians, but the guilt of the whole business will be laid upon us beyond a doubt, for it will not seem probable that Christians would have wished to do this kind of thing to a Christian, or Jews to do it to a Jew. What then is likely to come out but the truth of the matter? and the detection of the truth will bring a very extreme peril upon us all. Indeed, through the fault of our imprudence, and not undeservedly, our race will be utterly driven out from all parts of England, and—which is even more to be dreaded—we, our wives and our little ones will be given over as a prey to the barbarians, we shall be delivered up to death, we shall be exterminated, and our name will become a reproach to all people for ever. We ought therefore to take counsel warily for averting the approach of so many threatening mischiefs, and we must enter upon a different course from that which we have thought of. Look to yourselves then, say I, and acquiesce in my advice. Since the facts are as they are, and what is done cannot be undone, the first thing is to take measures whereby the matter may be concealed from the Christians, and so that may not happen which we fear. Briefly I say that the body must be put away from us and be exposed in some place a long way off from us, so that if it be found the Christians may think it a case of murder;[1] and if the talk of a murder becomes bruited abroad there is no doubt that the officers of the king's justices, eager for gain, will readily open their ears to the

---

1 *a case of murder* I.e., criminal homicide as opposed to religious ritual.

false rumour. Then, since the blame will be laid upon the Christians, it will make us safe."

[...]

[Book 2.] xi. The Fifth Argument [that the author's account is truthful]. As a proof of the truth and credibility of the matter we now adduce something which we have heard from the lips of Theobald, who was once a Jew, and afterwards a monk. He verily told us that in the ancient writings of his fathers it was written that the Jews, without the shedding of human blood, could neither obtain their freedom, nor could they ever return to their fatherland. Hence it was laid down by them in ancient times that every year they must sacrifice a Christian in some part of the world to the Most High God in scorn and contempt of Christ, that so they might avenge their sufferings on Him; inasmuch as it was because of Christ's death that they had been shut out from their own country, and were in exile as slaves in a foreign land.[1] Wherefore the chief men and Rabbis of the Jews who dwell in Spain assemble together at Narbonne, where the Royal seed [resides], and where they are held in the highest estimation, and they cast lots for all the countries which the Jews inhabit; and whatever country the lot falls upon, its metropolis has to carry out the same method with the other towns and cities, and the place whose lot is drawn has to fulfil the duty imposed by authority.[2] Now in that year in which we know that William, God's glorious martyr, was slain, it happened that the lot fell upon the Norwich Jews, and all the synagogues in England signified, by letter or by message, their consent that the wickedness should be carried out at Norwich. "I was," said he, "at that time at Cambridge, a Jew among Jews, and the commission of the crime was no secret to me. But in process of time, as I became acquainted with the glorious display of miracles which the divine power carried out through the merits of the blessed martyr William, I became much

---

1   *because of Christ's death ... land*   Refers to the aftermath of the destruction of the Second Temple in 70 CE and the beginning of the Diaspora, which *Siege* also describes at lines 1317–24.

2   *Wherefore the chief men ... authority*   A conspiracy theory that imagines Jewish religious hierarchy on a model similar to the centralized religious authority of Rome and the papal court. The fantasy of a "Jewish Pope of Narbonne" was first recorded by English historian William of Malmesbury c. 1140.

afraid, and following the dictates of my conscience, I forsook Judaism, and turned to the Christian faith."

These words, observe—the words of a converted Jew—we reckon to be all the truer, in that we received them as uttered by one who was a converted enemy, and also had been privy to the secrets of our enemies.

3. Ecclesiastical and Secular Legal Documents

a. from Pope Innocent III, Canons and Decrees of the Fourth Lateran Council[1] (1215)

> The Fourth Lateran Council, the most important ecumenical council of the Middle Ages, was held at the Lateran Palace in Rome in November 1215, near the end of the papacy of Innocent III. It was attended by thousands and produced a series of canons and decrees concerning a variety of issues, most famously related to Innocent III's plans for a new crusade to retake the Holy Land (lost since 1187), the morality of clergy, doctrine pertaining to the Eucharist and the sacrament of confession, the suppression of heresy, and the treatment of Jews and Muslims in Christian lands. The excerpts below include what applies directly to Jews. While these canons mostly reaffirm older papal opinions, they effectively communicate the preoccupations of medieval ecclesiastical and secular legislation concerning Jewish populations in Christendom: social and professional segregation of Jews and, especially, economic tensions related to moneylending.

CONCERNING THE INTEREST TAKEN BY JEWS

The more the Christian religion is restrained in the exaction of interest[2] so much more does the knavery of the Jews in this matter increase, so that in a short time they exhaust the wealth of Christians. Wishing therefore to provide for Christians in this matter lest they be burdened excessively by the Jews, we ordain through synodal decree that if they hereafter extort heavy and unrestrained interest,

---

1 *Canons and Decrees of the Fourth Lateran Council* English text from Marcus, ed. and trans., *The Jew in the Medieval World*, 153–57.
2 *the Christian religion ... interest* The medieval church strongly condemned the lending of money or goods at interest.

no matter what the pretext be, Christians shall be withdrawn from association with them until the Jews give adequate satisfaction for their unmitigated oppression. Also the Christians shall be compelled, if necessary, through Church punishment from which an appeal will be disregarded, to abstain from business relations with the Jews.

Moreover, we command the princes that they should not be hostile to the Christians because of this,[1] but should rather seek to restrain the Jews from so great an oppression.

And under threat of the same penalty we decree that Jews should be compelled to make good the tithes and dues owed to the churches which the churches have been accustomed to receive from the houses and other possessions of the Christians before they came into the possession of the Jews,[2] regardless of the circumstances, so that the Church be preserved against loss.

That Jews Should Be Distinguished from Christians in Dress

In some provinces a difference in dress distinguishes the Jews or Saracens[3] from the Christians, but in certain others such a confusion has grown up that they cannot be distinguished by any difference. Thus it happens at times that through error Christians have relations with the women of Jews or Saracens, and Jews or Saracens with Christian women. Therefore, that they may not, under pretext of error of this sort, excuse themselves in the future for the excesses of such prohibited intercourse, we decree that such Jews and Saracens of both sexes in every Christian province and at all times shall be marked off in the eyes of the public from other peoples through the character of their dress. Particularly, since it may be read in the writings of Moses that this very law has been enjoined upon them.[4]

Moreover, during the last three days before Easter and especially on Good Friday, they shall not go forth in public at all, for the reason that

---

1   *the princes ... because of this*   I.e., secular powers should not resent the church's interference in regional economies (where they might see profit from various investments and creditor arrangements).

2   *tithes and dues ... the Jews*   I.e., money pledged to the church (traditionally a tenth of annual earnings) when Christians owned the houses or possessions.

3   *Saracens*   Muslims.

4   *it may be read ... upon them*   Refers to Numbers 15.37–40. Many ecclesiastical and secular laws mandating a Jewish "badge of shame" were issued before and after the Fourth Lateran Council. The exact nature of the badge differed according to regional legislation.

some of them on these very days, as we hear, do not blush to go forth better dressed[1] and are not afraid to mock the Christians who maintain the memory of the most holy Passion by wearing signs of mourning.

This, however, we forbid most severely, that any one should presume at all to break forth in insult to the Redeemer. And since we ought not to ignore any insult to Him who blotted out our disgraceful deeds, we command that such impudent fellows be checked by the secular princes by imposing on them proper punishment so that they shall not at all presume to blaspheme Him who was crucified for us.

THAT JEWS NOT BE APPOINTED TO PUBLIC OFFICES

Since it would be altogether too absurd that a blasphemer of Christ should exercise authority over Christians, we, in this chapter, renew, because of the boldness of transgressors, what the Toledo Council has prudently decreed in this matter. We forbid that Jews be preferred for public offices since by pretext of some sort they manifest as much hostility to Christians as possible. If, moreover, any one should thus turn over an office to them, after due warning he shall be checked by a severe punishment, as is fit, by the provincial council which we command to meet every year. Indeed, the association of Christians with such a Jewish official in commercial and other matters shall not be allowed until whatever he has gotten from Christians through the office is transferred to the use of poor Christians, as the diocesan bishop shall carefully direct. And he shall be dismissed in disgrace from the office which he has impiously assumed. We extend the application of this law also to pagans.[2]

CONVERTS TO THE FAITH FROM AMONG THE JEWS MUST NOT OBSERVE THE OLD CUSTOMS OF THE JEWS

Some converted Jews, as we understand, who came voluntarily to the waters of Holy Baptism, have not altogether sloughed off the old man in order to put on the new man more perfectly. Since they retain remnants of their earlier rites they confound the majesty of the Christian religion through such a mixture. Since, moreover, it is written:

---

1 *better dressed* Than usual, or than Christians would be during Holy Week, traditionally a time of mourning the suffering and death of Christ.

2 *pagans* I.e., any non-Christian.

"Woe unto the man that goeth on the earth two ways,"[1] and since one ought not to put on a garment woven of both linen and wool,[2] we therefore ordain that such persons must be restrained in every way by the prelates of the churches from the observance of their old religious rites. For in the observance of Christianity it is necessary that a healthy compulsion should preserve these Jews whom free will has carried to the Christian religion. It is a lesser evil not to know the way of the Lord than to go back, after it has been acknowledged.

THE EXPEDITION TO RECOVER THE HOLY LAND[3]

... If any of those setting out thither[4] are bound by oath to pay interest, we command that their creditors shall be compelled by the same means[5] to release them from their oaths and to desist from the exaction of interest. But if any creditor shall compel them to pay interest, we order that he shall be forced, by a similar chastisement, to pay it back.

We command that the Jews, however, shall be compelled by the secular power to remit interest; and until they remit it all faithful Christians shall, under penalty of excommunication, refrain from every species of intercourse with them. For those, moreover, who are unable at present to pay their debts to the Jews, the secular princes shall provide a useful delay, so that after they[6] begin their journey they shall suffer no inconvenience from interest, until their death or return is known with certainty. The Jews shall be compelled, after deducting the necessary expenses, to count the income which they receive in the meantime from the mortgaged property toward the payment of the principal;[7] since a favor of this kind, which defers the payment and does not cancel the debt, does not seem to cause much loss. Moreover let the prelates of the Church who are proven to be negligent in doing

---

1   *"Woe unto ... two ways"*   Sirach 2.12.

2   *one ought not ... wool*   Leviticus 19.19.

3   THE EXPEDITION ... HOLY LAND   What follows this heading is just a small excerpt from a larger set of decrees related to preparation of a new crusade.

4   *thither*   To the Holy Land.

5   *the same means*   I.e., the punishment of the church.

6   *they*   Those setting out to the Holy Land, i.e., crusaders.

7   *The Jews shall be ... principal*   I.e., if a Jewish lender receives income on possessions mortgaged against a debt while the debtor is away on crusade, that income will be deducted from the original amount borrowed.

justice to the crusaders and their families, understand that they shall be severely punished.

b. A Bull of Pope Gregory X[1] (1272)

The text of Pope Gregory X's bull (a papal edict, from Latin *bullum* or "seal") is in most ways a simple reissue of longstanding papal policies on the treatment of Jews. Called the *Sicut Judaeis* (Latin: "As the Jews," for the opening words of the edict proper), this type of bull was issued first by Calixtus II c. 1119–20 but even then evoked policy that went back to the sixth century. Gregory X's version includes a defense of Jews against ritual murder and blood libels. Such accusations (like those made in the William of Norwich case, above) were widespread by the end of the thirteenth century, and Gregory was compelled here to restate a refutation first explicitly articulated by Innocent IV in 1247.

Gregory, bishop, servant of the servants of God, extends greetings and the apostolic benediction to the beloved sons in Christ, the faithful Christians, to those here now and to those in the future. Even as it is not allowed to the Jews in their assemblies presumptuously to undertake for themselves more than that which is permitted them by law, even so they ought not to suffer any disadvantage in those[2] which have been granted them. Although they prefer to persist in their stubbornness rather than to recognize the words of their prophets and the mysteries of the Scriptures, and thus to arrive at a knowledge of Christian faith and salvation; nevertheless, inasmuch as they have made an appeal for our protection and help, we therefore admit their petition and offer them the shield of our protection through the clemency of Christian piety. In so doing we follow in the footsteps of our predecessors of blessed memory, the popes of Rome—Calixtus, Eugene, Alexander, Clement, Celestine, Innocent, and Honorius.[3]

---

1   *A Bull of Pope Gregory X*   English text from Marcus, ed. and trans., *The Jew in the Medieval World*, 170–72.

2   *those*   I.e., those privileges or permissions.

3   *we follow ... and Honorius*   Gregory confirms the reiterative nature of the bull, citing Popes Calixtus II (1119–24), Eugene III (1145–53), Alexander III (1159–81), Clement III (1187–91), Celestine III (1191–98), Innocent III (1198–1216), and Honorius III (1216–27).

We decree moreover that no Christian shall compel them or any one of their group to come to baptism unwillingly. But if any one of them shall take refuge of his own accord with Christians, because of conviction, then, after his intention will have been manifest, he shall be made a Christian without any intrigue. For, indeed, that person who is known to have come to Christian baptism not freely, but unwillingly, is not believed to possess the Christian faith.

Moreover no Christian shall presume to seize, imprison, wound, torture, mutilate, kill, or inflict violence on them; furthermore no one shall presume, except by judicial action of the authorities of the country, to change the good customs in the land where they live for the purpose of taking their money or goods from them or from others.

In addition, no one shall disturb them in any way during the celebration of their festivals, whether by day or by night, with clubs or stones or anything else. And no one shall exact any compulsory service of them unless it be that which they have been accustomed to render in previous times.

Inasmuch as the Jews are not able to bear witness against the Christians, we decree furthermore that the testimony of Christians against Jews shall not be valid unless there is among these Christians some Jew who is there for the purpose of offering testimony.[1]

Since it happens occasionally that some Christians lose their Christian children, the Jews are accused by their enemies of secretly carrying off and killing these same Christian children and of making sacrifices of the heart and blood of these very children.[2] It happens, too, that the parents of these children or some other Christian enemies of these Jews, secretly hide these very children in order that they may be able to injure these Jews, and in order that they may be able to extort from them a certain amount of money by redeeming them from their straits.

And most falsely do these Christians claim that the Jews have secretly and furtively carried away these children and killed them, and

---

1 *testimony of Christians ... offering testimony* I.e., a Jew should not be convicted of a crime if there is only Christian testimony against him or her.

2 *Since it happens ... children* Refers to accusations of ritual murder, often paired with accusations of ritual shedding, collection, or consumption of blood. Cf. Thomas of Monmouth's account of the convert Theobald's testimony in the William of Norwich case, above.

that the Jews offer sacrifice from the heart and the blood of these children, since their law in this matter precisely and expressly forbids Jews to sacrifice, eat, or drink the blood, or to eat the flesh of animals having claws.[1] This has been demonstrated many times at our court by Jews converted to the Christian faith: nevertheless very many Jews are often seized and detained unjustly because of this.

We decree, therefore, that Christians need not be obeyed against Jews in a case or situation of this type, and we order that Jews seized under such a silly pretext be freed from imprisonment, and that they shall not be arrested henceforth on such a miserable pretext, unless— which we do not believe—they be caught in the commission of the crime. We decree that no Christian shall stir up anything new against them, but that they should be maintained in that status and position in which they were in the time of our predecessors, from antiquity till now.

We decree, in order to stop the wickedness and avarice of bad men, that no one shall dare to devastate or to destroy a cemetery of the Jews or to dig up human bodies for the sake of getting money. Moreover, if any one, after having known the content of this decree, should— which we hope will not happen—attempt audaciously to act contrary to it, then let him suffer punishment in his rank and position, or let him be punished by the penalty of excommunication, unless he makes amends for his boldness by proper recompense. Moreover, we wish that only those Jews who have not attempted to contrive anything toward the destruction of the Christian faith be fortified by the support of such protection....

Given at Orvieto by the hand of the Magister John Lectator, vice-chancellor of the Holy Roman Church, on the 7th of October, in the first indiction,[2] in the year 1272 of the divine incarnation, in the first year of the pontificate of our master, the Pope Gregory X.

---

1   *their law ... having claws*   Refers to Jewish dietary laws (kashrut), specifically those set down in Leviticus 11.3–8 and Deuteronomy 14.4–8.
2   *indiction*   Fifteen-year cycle.

c. Statute of the Jewry, England (1275)

> Edward I's Statute of the Jewry was issued in Anglo-Norman French, probably at Easter 1275 (the original *Les Estatutz de la Jewerie* is available in the 1810 *Statutes of the Realm* from which the translation below is also taken). It marks the king's attempt to address Jewish moneylending, wealth, and royal protection early in his reign. While Jewish merchants were invited to England by William the Conqueror in 1070, and were always accountable only to the king, English Jews could not own land or participate in trade. Since church disapproval of profiting from interest on financial transactions effectively banned the practice for Christians, however, Jewish money-lending fulfilled an important economic role for both Jews and Christians. It also bred resentment. The tensions and vindictiveness caused by the resulting creditor-debtor relationships and mixed religio-economic anxieties are clear in William of Newburgh's account of the 1190 York massacre (above), as they are reflected in the focus on financial transaction in Thomas of Monmouth's account of the abduction of William of Norwich (above) and in the *Siege*'s scenes of looted wealth from Jerusalem in lines 1165–72 and 1265–80. The 1275 Statute forbid English Jews from lending money at interest, cutting off many from their living, and attempted to substitute new rights: land ownership, legal trade, and farming and agricultural endeavors. It simultaneously reiterated ongoing marginalization and segregation of Jews. It was unsuccessful.

FORASMUCH as the King hath seen that divers Evils, and the disheriting of the good Men of his Land have happened by the Usuries[1] which the Jews have made in Time past, and that divers Sins have followed thereupon; albeit he and his Ancestors have received much benefit from the Jewish People in all Time past; nevertheless for the Honour of God and the common benefit of the People, the King hath ordained and established, That from henceforth no Jew shall lend any Thing at Usury,[2] either upon Land, or upon Rent, or upon other Thing: And that no usuries shall run[3] in Time coming from the Feast

---

1   *Usuries*   Interest rates charged on debts.
2   *at Usury*   With interest rates applied.
3   *run*   Accrue.

of Saint Edward[1] last past. Nothwithstanding, the Covenants[2] before made shall be observed, saving[3] that the Usuries shall cease. But all those who owe Debts to Jews upon Pledges of Moveables,[4] shall acquit them[5] between this and Easter; if not they shall be forfeited.[6] And if any Jew shall lend at Usury contrary to this Ordinance, the King will not lend his Aid, neither by himself nor his Officers, for the recovering of his Loan; but will punish him at his discretion for the Offence, and will do justice to the Christian that he may obtain his Pledge[7] again.

AND that the Distresses[8] for Debts due unto the Jews from henceforth shall not be so grievous, but that the Moiety[9] of the Lands and Chattels of the Christians shall remain for their Maintenance; and that no Distress shall be made for a Jewry Debt upon the Heir of the Debtor named in the Jew's Deed, nor upon any other Person holding the Land that was the Debtor's, before that the Debt be put in Suit[10] and allowed in Court.

And if the Sheriff or other Bailiff, by the King's Command hath to give Seisin[11] to a Jew, be it one or more, for their Debt, of Chattels or Land to the Value of the Debt, the Chattels shall be valued by the Oaths of good Men, and be delivered to the Jew or Jews, or to their Proxy, to the Amount of the Debt; and if the Chattels be not sufficient, the Lands shall be extended[12] by the same Oath before the Delivery of Seisin to the Jew or Jews, to each in his due Proportion; so that it may be certainly known that the Debt is quit, and the Christian may have his Land again:[13] Saving always to the Christian

---

1 *Feast of Saint Edward* Probably St. Edward the Martyr, whose feast day is 18 March (Edward the Confessor and 13 October is the alternative).
2 *Covenants* Contracts, financial agreements.
3 *saving* Except.
4 *Pledges of Moveables* Goods (moveable property) pledged as security for repayment.
5 *acquit them* Pay the debts.
6 *they shall be forfeited* I.e., the goods pledged as security will be given up (because the loan will have defaulted).
7 *his Pledge* I.e., the forfeited goods.
8 *Distresses* Seizures of property or land to compel payment.
9 *Moiety* Half part.
10 *be put in Suit* Is sued for by legal action.
11 *Seisin* Possession (of property in lieu of payment).
12 *extended* Levied.
13 *again* After the remaining debt has been collected by means of levy on the land.

the Moiety of his Land and Chattels for his maintenance as aforesaid, and the Chief Mansion.[1]

And if any Moveables hereafter be found in Possession of a Jew, and any Man shall sue him,[2] the Jew shall be allowed his warranty,[3] if he may have it; and if not, let him answer therefore: So that he be not herein otherwise[4] privileged than a Christian.

AND that all Jews shall dwell in the King's own Cities and Boroughs, where the Chests of Chirographs of Jewry are wont to be:[5] And that each Jew after he shall be Seven Years old, shall wear a Badge on his outer Garment; that is to say, in the Form of Two Tables joined,[6] of yellow Felt, of the Length of Six Inches, and of the Breadth of Three Inches. And that each one, after he shall be Twelve Years old, pay Three pence yearly at Easter of Tax to the King, whose Bondman he is; and this shall hold place[7] as well for a Woman as a Man.

And that no Jew shall have Power to infeoff another,[8] whether Jew or Christian, of Houses, Rents, or Tenements that he now hath, nor to alien[9] in any other Manner, nor to make Acquittance to[10] any Christian of his Debt without the especial License of the King, until the King shall have otherwise ordained therein.

AND, Forasmuch as it is the will and sufferance of Holy Church that they may live and be preserved, the King taketh them under his Protection, and granteth them his Peace; and willeth that they be safely preserved and defended by his Sheriffs and other Bailiffs, and by his Liege Men; and commandeth that none shall do them harm,

---

1 *Chief Mansion* Main residence.
2 *sue him* I.e., for the return of the goods.
3 *his warranty* Whatever security was contractually pledged to him.
4 *otherwise* Any differently.
5 *where the Chests ... to be* In regional centers that house official repositories (chests, or *archae* in Latin) of documents and contracts related to Jewish lending and business. Chirographs are documents made in duplicate or often triplicate, so that each interested party had a copy of the agreement while one copy would be preserved in the chest. The statute is restricting Jewish residence to places near the *archae*.
6 *a Badge ... Two Tables joined* The medieval English badge for Jews, mandated from 1217 in accordance with the canons of the Fourth Lateran Council (above), legislated that Jewish difference be marked by a likeness of the tablets of the Ten Commandments ("Two Tables," i.e., tablets).
7 *hold place* Apply.
8 *infeoff another* Grant rights or revenue (under the feudal system) to another person.
9 *alien* Force surrender or transfer of property.
10 *make Acquittance to* Acquit.

or damage, or wrong, in their Bodies or in their Goods, moveable or immoveable;[1] and that they shall neither plead nor be impleaded[2] in any Court, nor be challenged or troubled in any Court, except in the Court of the King, whose Bondmen[3] they are. And that none shall owe Obedience, or Service, or Rent, except to the King, or his Bailiffs in his Name; unless it be for their Dwellings which they now hold by paying Rent; saving the Right of the Holy Church.[4]

AND the King granteth unto them that they may gain their living by lawful Merchandise[5] and their Labour; and that they may have Intercourse with Christians, in order to carry on lawful Trade by selling and buying. But that no Christian, for this Cause or any other, shall dwell among them. And the King willeth that they shall not by reason of their Merchandise be put to Lot or Scot,[6] nor in Taxes with the Men of the Cities or Boroughs where they abide; for that they are taxable to the King as his Bondmen, and to none other but the King.

Moreover the King granteth unto them that they may buy Houses and Curtilages,[7] in the Cities and Boroughs where they abide, so that they hold them in chief of the King: saving unto the Lords of the Fee[8] their Services due and accustomed. And that they may take and buy Farms or Land for the Term of Ten Years or less, without taking Homages or Fealties,[9] or such sort of Obedience from Christians, and without having Advowsons[10] of Churches; and that they may be able to gain their living in the World, if they have not the Means of Trading, or cannot Labour; and this License to take Lands to farm shall endure to them only for Fifteen Years from this Time forward.[11]

---

1   *immoveable* E.g., houses or lands.
2   *impleaded* Sued.
3   *Bondmen* Serfs.
4   *saving ... Holy Church* I.e., the statute is not gainsaying privileges or properties of the church.
5   *Merchandise* Trading, i.e., Jews may trade and engage in legal commerce without charging interest on transactions.
6   *put to Lot or Scot* Subject to municipal taxation.
7   *Curtilages* Lands and buildings attached to houses.
8   *Lords of the Fee* Those who hold the property (with rights and revenues pertaining) by hereditary right and are due feudal obligations.
9   *Homages or Fealties* Oaths of allegiance or obligation to a lord.
10 *Advowsons* Property rights that allow the presentation or nomination of clergy to a benefice.
11 *Fifteen Years ... forward* I.e., until 1290.

4. Popular Literature: Miracles of the Virgin and Mandeville's *Travels*

a. "The Jewish Boy" and "Jews of Toledo," from *The South English Legendary*[1] (c. 1280)

> *The South English Legendary* is a Middle English collection of versi-
> fied saints' lives and homilies for feast days, similar in many ways to
> *The Golden Legend* (excerpted above). It can be dated in its earliest
> form to c. 1270–85, but it is not a stable text: it survives in more
> than 50 manuscripts from the late thirteenth through the fifteenth
> centuries, and the number and arrangement of items varies consider-
> ably between each. In the majority, however, a series of six "Miracles
> of the Virgin" (narratives that relate the miraculous intercession of the
> Virgin Mary) are appended to the story of "St. Theophilus," a figure
> known primarily for praying to the Virgin and receiving her inter-
> cession. Included below are the first and last miracle stories in that
> group of six. The original early Middle English is written in rhyming
> couplets made up of 14-syllable lines, but it has been translated here
> into Modern English prose.

In days past, in Bourges, a Jew's child often played, as children still
happily like to do, with Christian children. It happened one Easter
day that the children began to walk to church, as children will do
when the day requires it. The Jew's child went with them, and when
he entered the church he paid close attention to everything he saw
there. When his friends kneeled down and cried out to the image on
high,[2] he kneeled down also, and he did everything that he saw the
others do. He felt fitting wonder at the sight of the cross he gazed
upon intently. It seemed to him that his heart was most drawn to an
image of Our Lady.[3] He devoted himself to that very image, that he
might love it above all: after that first look, she never left his mind.

When the people went forward to take communion, God's flesh
and blood, that child went up with them and also did the good deed.

---

1   *The South English Legendary*   Modern English text copyright Adrienne Williams Boyarin
© 2013, translated from Charlotte D'Evelyn and Anna J. Mill, eds., *The South English
Legendary*. Early English Text Society O.S. 235 (London: Oxford UP, 1956) 227–38.
2   *image on high*   A crucifix or other image of Jesus.
3   *Our Lady*   The Virgin Mary.

There, with his companions, he accepted God's flesh and blood, and afterwards he made his way home. While they[1] headed home, his father and his mother were searching everywhere for him. They were happy when he arrived at home, because they had been worried. The father asked him where he had been, and he immediately told him what he had done at church and how it was that he had ended up there.

The father was nearly insane with anger. Right away he began to stoke his oven. When the fire was burning hot, he tossed that child into the middle of it and shut the mouth of the oven. The mother acted as if she had gone insane. When she saw her child burned, she let out a tormented wail. She ran frantically through the streets and cried out miserably. She told the people how it was, and about all that had happened to her. The people came immediately to the oven, surrounding it on all sides. They found that child sitting in the middle of it, and playing with the fire.

They asked him if he knew why the fire had not come near him. "Indeed," he said. "The beautiful woman that I saw in the church, who stood on high, up near the cross, and who, it seemed to me, also stood by the altar and beckoned me towards it when I took communion—she afterwards came to me here, and she took her head covering and embraced me with it so that no fire or heat came near me. I have never been so happy anywhere as I was there. I believe in her son, whom the Jews hung on the tree."[2]

The people seized the child's father and stoked the oven until it was hot, and they threw the lout right into the middle of it and burned him to ashes. The child and his mother, and many others, immediately accepted Christianity and believed in God and His mother and became good people. Otherwise, except for the miracle of that child, they would have been evildoers. One can yet tell more miracles concerning Our Lady sweet and mild.

[…]

---

1   *they* People who were in the church.
2   *tree* Cross.

Jews hate Our Lady intensely, and her precious son too. That is observable in many of the deeds the evildoers have done. Once at harvest time, on Our Lady's Day,[1] which is so holy and precious, a certain archbishop was singing his Mass in the city of Toledo. During the Mass, just at the point of the consecration,[2] at the very moment of that holy deed, he heard a voice from heaven that said these words: "Those evildoers will put Him on the cross once again, so viciously, and so shamefully hatefully, with such cruel intentions!" When the archbishop had brought the Mass to an end, he took a sufficiently large group of people with him and set out towards the Jewry, and he had them search everywhere. Finally they found a likeness of Our Lord on a cross, beaten and bound, nailed through the feet and hands, as Our Lord with His five wounds. The Jews had done this. May God grant suffering to them and to all who show love for them, for many are the vile and shameful acts that they often do to Our Lord in secret. Yet in the past Our Lady descended and warned this bishop. She has done great goodness ever since she was born. Now, Lady, for your mercy, which has ever been in you, and for the great sorrow that you had when your son died on a tree, grant us grace, so we might obtain that mercy here, so we might attain the joy that you dwell in.

b. "The Child Slain by Jews,"[3] from the Vernon Manuscript (c. 1390)

> The Vernon Manuscript (named for a seventeenth-century owner) is a very large compendium of late-fourteenth-century English poetry and prose. It comprises about 370 texts by many authors and in many genres, and it once contained a collection of 41 illustrated Miracles of the Virgin. Only eight of those survive in full, and they include another version of the "The Jewish Boy" (above) and the tale excerpted here. "The Child Slain by Jews" is an analogue of Chaucer's better-known "Prioress's Tale" (from *The Canterbury Tales*), a version of a very common miracle story known in more than 30 versions and seven languages in the Middle Ages. It shares plot elements with Thomas of

---

1   *Our Lady's Day*   The Feast of the Nativity of the Virgin Mary, 8 September.
2   *consecration*   I.e., of the bread and wine of communion.
3   "*The Child Slain by Jews*"   Modern English text copyright Adrienne Williams Boyarin © 2013, translated from Carl Horstmann, ed., *The Minor Poems of the Vernon MS.* Early English Text Society O.S. 98 (London: Kegan Paul, 1892), 141–45.

Monmouth's account of the murder of William of Norwich (above), and its description of the lamenting mother might be read comparatively with the mothers in *The Passion of William of Norwich*, "The Jewish Boy," and *Siege* lines 1081–1100. Originally written in Middle English octosyllabic couplets and accompanied by a fine illustration of its content, the tale is provided here in a Modern English prose translation.

How the Jews, to spite Our Lady, threw a child into a privy.[1]

Whoever loves Our Lady well, she will indeed reward him what he desires, either during his lifetime or at the time of his death. The Lady is so generous and kind. It happened once in Paris, as stories in sacred writings[2] attest—in that city, this incident occurred.

A poor beggar child, who through begging supported his family somewhat—his father, his mother, and also himself—went begging through every part of the city. The child knew no skills, except to win his sustenance with his mouth. The child's singing voice was pleasant and clear. Men listened to his song very happily. From street to street, he got his food through his song, which was very pleasant. Men heard his song with great pleasure. It was a hymn about Our Lady: everywhere he went he sung the hymn called *Alma redemptoris mater*,[3] which means, to put it plainly: "Mother of God, gentle and pure, gate of heaven and star of the sea, save your people from sin and misery." That song was considered beautiful. The child sang it from house to house. Because he sang it so delightfully, the Jews harbored enmity towards him, until it happened on one Saturday that the child's path led through the Jewry. The Jews hated that song. Therefore, they plotted for the child to be murdered. The child sang there so delightfully. He had never before sung so cheerfully.

One of the malicious Jews lured the child into his house. He revealed his malice there: he immediately slit the child's throat. The child did not leave off because of that evil but continued singing his song nevertheless. Whenever he finished, he began again. No one

---

1 *How the Jews ... privy* I.e., into a latrine. This title survives in a contents list that is contemporary with the manuscript.

2 *sacred writings* Respected religious writings, not scripture.

3 *Alma redemptoris mater* Latin: "Loving Mother of the Redeemer," the first words of the hymn. The poet goes on to give a loose translation of its first sentence.

could stop his singing. The Jew was grievously troubled therefore. Lest his malicious deed be discovered, the Jew figured out a trick: he tossed the child down deep into the privy pit that was there. The child continued singing the same song. So cheerfully the child could shout out! He had never sung so loudly before. Men could hear him near and far. The child's voice was so loud and clear.

The child's mother was in the habit of waiting everyday until noon, when he was in the habit of bringing home food, whatever he could get with his singing. But on that day the hour passed. His mother was therefore horribly anxious. With sorrow and sigh, through every street, she searched for the place where she might find him. But when she entered the Jewry, she heard his voice, so clear in its call. The mother moved toward that voice. By it, she knew where he was.

Then straightaway she asked about her child. The Jew immediately denied any knowledge of him and said there was no such child there. Still the child's mother would not stop, and the mother cried on endlessly. The Jew endlessly said there was no such person. Then the woman said, "You speak incorrectly. He is in there. I know his song." The Jew began to stare and swear oaths and said that no such child had come there. But nevertheless people could hear the child singing continuously, strong and clear, and always more and more, higher and higher. Men could here him both near and far.

The mother knew no other hope: she goes[1] to the mayor and bailiffs; she complains that the Jew has committed a crime against her by stealing her son because of his song; she begs them to give her justice and judgment, to bring her son into her sight; she begs the mayor, *par charité*,[2] to grant her legal possession[3] of him; and meanwhile she tells the mayor how she survives by means of her son's song. Then the mayor takes pity on her and calls upon the people of that city. He tells them about the women's words and says he must do justice by her, and he commands them to accompany him in order to bring the woman's case to an end.

When they arrived there, they immediately hear the child's voice, even over all of their noise. It was just like an angel's voice. They had

---

1   *she goes*   The poet writes in the historical present tense for this section, a dramatic device.
2   *par charité*   French: out of kindness.
3   *legal possession*   The term in Middle English is *freo lyvere* (free livery), i.e., a voluntary legal transfer of property.

never heard him sing so clearly. There the mayor entered and request-ed delivery of the child. The Jew could not refuse the mayor, nor clear himself of blame regarding the child, but instead had to acknowledge his crime, proven guilty by the child's song. The mayor searched for him a long time, until he was found in the privy, completely deeply drowned in the filth of excrement. Then the mayor commanded that the child, so foully spattered with excrement and filth, be lifted up— and also the child's throat was cut open.[1] Right then, before they did anything else, the Jew was convicted of that murder. And before the people scattered, the bishop arrived to see that miracle.

In the presence of the bishop and all gathered, the child continued to sing equally clearly. The bishop searched with his hand: inside the child's throat, he found a lily flower, so beautiful and bright. So fair a lily had never been seen before, with golden letters all over it: *Alma redemptoris mater*. As soon as that lily was removed, the child's song began to cease. That pleasant song was heard no more, and instead the child lay there as a dead body.

With great ceremony, the bishop had the body carried through the whole city, and, in procession, he himself went with the body through the whole town, with priests and clerks who knew how to sing, and he commanded them to ring all the bells. With burning candles and magnificent vestments, they led that holy body honorably, as they processed, into the church and began the Requiem Mass, as is cus-tomary for the dead. But just then they were interrupted: the corpse rose up in their presence and began the *Salve sancta parens*.[2] Men could well understand by this that the child had served Our Sweet Lady, who had so honored him here on earth and carried his soul to a bliss so pure.

Therefore I advise that every man serve that Lady as well as he can, and love her with his best efforts. She will reward him well for his service. Now, Mary, on account of your great strength, help us into heaven, which is so bright!

---

1 *the child's throat ... open* I.e., they discovered that the child's throat was cut.
2 *Salve sancta parens* Latin: "Hail holy parent," another well-known prayer to the Virgin Mary.

c. "How a Monk Painted a Miraculous Image,"[1] from John Mirk's *Festial* (c. 1390)

> Mirk's *Festial* is an influential Middle English prose collection of sermons, organized around the Christian liturgical year. John Mirk, an Augustinian canon at Lilleshall Abbey in Shropshire, probably composed most of it in the 1380s, though nearly 40 later manuscripts survive, in various forms, and the work was printed repeatedly in the fifteenth and sixteenth centuries. The brief excerpt here is an *exemplum* (example), a short moralizing tale used to illustrate or support the message of a sermon. It was likely intended as a set-piece for feast days associated with the Virgin Mary, though in its manuscript settings it follows a related tale about a monk who wrote Miracles of the Virgin and is not attached to any particular sermon or feast day.

And so the monk traveled to Jerusalem on pilgrimage, and also to many other good holy places. And so one day he and a Jew, who was a great scholar in that land, sat together and spoke about Our Lady. And so the Jew said that a virgin could never give birth to a child, and the monk said, "Yes," and so they argued intensely about it. And so finally, since the monk praised Our Lady so passionately and so often, the Jew asked him to paint an image of her on a piece of wood so that he might take a look at the image. And he painted a wondrously beautiful image of Our Lady with her child in her arm, and with a pretty little nipple on her breast. And then the Jew gazed intently at her, and he thought her very beautiful. And so he asked the monk whether she had been as beautiful as he made her, and the monk said, "Yes, and twenty times more beautiful than any man could make her." And then as the Jew stood there and looked at her, the child that was in her arm lifted his head away from the piece of wood and took his mother's breast in his hand and squeezed out milk and sucked on it. And when the Jew saw that, he kneeled down and thanked God and

---

1   *"How a Monk Painted a Miraculous Image"*   Modern English text copyright Adrienne Williams Boyarin © 2013, translated from Theodor Erbe, ed., *Mirk's Festial: A Collection of Homilies by Johannes Mirkus*. Early English Text Society E.S. 96 (London: Kegan Paul, 1905), 302–03.

cried out for mercy from Our Lady, and he said he knew well that it was a lesser miracle for a virgin to give birth to a child than for that image, which was painted on a piece of wood, to lift up its head from the wood, and also for that breast to give milk. And so the Jew was baptized and converted to the faith, and he turned many others into Christians.

d. from *The Travels of Sir John Mandeville*[1] (c.1360)

> *The Travels of Sir John Mandeville* was an exceptionally popular travel narrative in the late-medieval and early-modern periods (more than 275 manuscripts survive, in 10 languages), ostensibly written by an English knight from St. Albans who set out on pilgrimage to Jerusalem in 1322. The work tells of his travels through Europe to the Holy Land and then throughout Asia in fantastical and often racially- and religiously-charged ways. It is clear that "John Mandeville" is a fictive pseudonym (the identity of the author remains unknown), and that the work finds its sources not so much in travel experience as in legend, history, romance, and prophecy. The section excerpted here is its account of the 10 lost tribes of Israel and the apocalyptic threat of Jewish linguistic and national unity. Many traditions (within Judaism, Christianity, and Islam) have similar stories about the purportedly "lost tribes" who disappeared with the destruction of the ancient kingdom of Israel by the Assyrians in the eighth century BCE.

In that same region[2] ben[3] the mountains of Caspia that men clepen[4] "Uber"[5] in the country. Between those mountains the Jews of ten

---

1   *The Travels of Sir John Mandeville*   The passage below follows British Library manuscript Cotton Titus C.xvi (c. 1400–25), but the Middle English has been lightly modernized for inclusion in the present volume. For an excellent Modern English translation of the full work, see John Mandeville, *The Book of Marvels and Travels*, ed. and trans. Anthony Bale (Oxford: Oxford UP, 2012).

2   *that same region*   This chapter begins with discussion of the "Caldilhe" region, thought to be a Tartar kingdom on the Volga River, near the Caucasus mountain range.

3   *ben*   Are.

4   *clepen*   Call.

5   *Uber*   From Latin: *ubera aquilonis*, the breasts of the north wind.

lineages[1] ben enclosed, that men clepen Goth and Magoth;[2] and they may not go out on no side. There were enclosed twenty two kings with their people, that dwelled between the mountains of Sythia.[3] There King Alexander[4] chased them between those mountains; and there he thought for to enclose them through work of his men. But when he saw that he might not do it, nor bring it to an end, he prayed to God of nature that He would perform that that he had begun. And all were it so that he was a paynim[5] and not worthy to be heard, yet God of His grace closed the mountains together; so that they dwell there, all fast locked and enclosed with high mountains all about, save only on one side; and on that side is the Sea of Caspia.[6] Now may some men ask: since that the sea is on that one side, wherefore go they not out on the sea side, for to go where that them liketh?[7] But to this question I shall answer: that Sea of Caspia goeth out by land, under the mountains, and runneth by the desert at one side of the country; and after it stretcheth unto the ends of Persia. And although it be clept a sea, it is no sea, ne it toucheth to none[8] other sea; but it is a lake, the greatest of the world. And though they would put them[9] into that sea, they ne wisten never[10] where that they should arrive. And also they can no language but only their own, that no man knoweth but they;[11] and therefore may they not go out. And also ye shall understand that the Jews have no proper land of their own, for to dwell in, in all the world, but only that land between the mountains. And yet they yield tribute for

---

1 *lineages* Tribes.

2 *Goth and Magoth* Gog and Magog, names of devils in Christian legendary traditions, but associated with apocalyptic battles in Ezekiel 38–39 and Revelation 20.7–8. The names also appear separately in genealogies at Genesis 10.2 (Magog) and 1 Chronicles 5.4 (Gog).

3 *Sythia* Northern Caucasus.

4 *King Alexander* Alexander the Great.

5 *all were ... paynim* Even though he was a pagan.

6 *Sea of Caspia* An inland sea of Central Asia.

7 *where that them liketh* Wherever they please.

8 *ne it toucheth to none* Nor does it meet with any.

9 *though they would put them* Even if they wanted to set out.

10 *ne wisten never* Do not ever know.

11 *can no language ... but they* I.e., they do not know any language other than their own (Hebrew), which nobody else speaks.

that land to the queen of Amazona,[1] the which that maketh them to ben[2] kept in close[3] full diligently, that they shall not go out on no side, but by the coast of their land; for their land marcheth to[4] those mountains. And often it hath befallen that some of the Jews have gone up the mountains, and avaled[5] down to the valleys: but great number of folk ne may not[6] do so. For the mountains ben so high, and so straight up, that they must abide there, maugre[7] their might. For they may not go out, but by a little issue[8] that was made by strength of men; and it lasteth well a four great mile. And after is there yet a land all desert, where men may find no water, ne for digging ne for none other thing:[9] wherefore men may not dwell in that place. So is it full of dragons, of serpents, and of other venomous beasts, that no man dare not pass, but if it be strong winter. And that strait[10] passage men clepen in that country "Clyron." And that is the passage that the Queen of Amazona maketh to be kept. And though it happen some of them, by fortune, to go out,[11] they can no manner of language but Hebrew, so that they cannot speak to the people. And yet nonetheless, men say they shall go out in the time of Antichrist, and that they shall make great slaughter of Christian men. And therefore all the Jews that dwell in all lands learn always to speak Hebrew, in hope that when the other Jews shall go out, that they may understand their speech, and to lead them into Christendom for to destroy the Christian people. For the Jews say that they know well by their prophecies that they of Caspia shall go out and spread throughout all the world; and that the Christian men shall be under their subjection as long as[12] they have been in subjection of

---

1   *Amazona*   A legendary territory that the Mandeville author places adjacent to the "Caldilhe" region described above.
2   *the which ... to ben*   Who makes sure they are.
3   *in close*   Enclosed.
4   *marcheth to*   Borders upon, sits up against.
5   *avaled*   Descended.
6   *ne may not*   Are not able to.
7   *maugre*   In spite of.
8   *issue*   Way out.
9   *ne for digging ... other thing*   Neither by digging nor by any other means.
10 *strait*   Narrow.
11 *though it happen ... go out*   Even if by chance some of them get out.
12 *as long as*   For the same amount of time that.

them. And if that you will wit[1] how that they shall find their way, after that[2] I have heard say, I shall tell you. In the time of Antichrist, a fox shall make there his train,[3] and mine[4] a hole, where King Alexander let make the gates:[5] and so long he shall mine and pierce the earth, till that he shall pass through towards that folk. And when they see the fox, they shall have great marvel of him, because that they saw never such a beast. For of all other beasts they have enclosed amongst them, save only[6] the fox. And then they shall chase him and pursue him so strait, till that he come to the same place that he came from. And then they shall dig and mine so strongly, till that they find the gates that King Alexander let make of great stones and passing[7] huge, well cemented and made strong for the mastery.[8] And those gates they shall break, and so go out, by finding of that issue.

5. Christian Dates in Relation to the Destruction of the Second Temple: A Jewish Response, from Abraham Zacuto, *Book of Lineage*[9] (c. 1500)

Abraham ben Samuel Zacuto (1452–1515?) was a Spanish rabbi, astronomer, and historian who lived through the expulsions and persecutions of Jews associated with the Inquisition. His *Sefer Yuhasin* (*Book of Lineage*) is an account of Jewish law and history from creation to the year 1500, some of which is devoted to Jewish-Christian polemics. It was composed over many years and was likely not completed until 1504. In the short excerpt included here, Abraham responds to the Christian dating of the birth and death of Jesus, and particularly to the polemical relationship of this dating to the de-

---

1 *that you will wit*   You want to know.
2 *after that*   In accordance with what.
3 *train*   Burrow.
4 *mine*   Dig.
5 *let make the gates*   Had the gates built.
6 *save only*   Except.
7 *passing*   Exceedingly.
8 *for the mastery*   To the utmost degree.
9 *Book of Lineage*   English text copyright Shamma A. Boyarin © 2013, translated from the Hebrew as it appears in Abraham ben Samuel Zacuto, *Sefer Yuhasin ha-Shalem* (Jerusalem: Yerid ha-Sefarim, 2004), 20.

struction of the Second Temple. Though usually internally coherent within the *Sefer Yuhasin*, many of Abraham's dates are not related to currently accepted dating practices. However, the point he makes is clear: there are multiple ways to date ancient historical events, and there are discrepancies, often related to religious polemics, between different traditions.

The truth is that the Nazarene[1] was born in the fourth year of the rule of Yannai II, who is Alexander,[2] which was the year two hundred and sixty-three from the rebuilding of the Temple,[3] and the fifty-first year of the Hasmoneans,[4] which is the year three thousand six hundred and seventy-eight since creation,[5] even though the Christians say he was born at the time of Herod, the servant of the Hasmoneans,[6] that is, in the year [three thousand] seven hundred and sixty[7] since creation, and that he was hung thirty-five years before the destruction,[8] at the age of thirty-two. Their intent is to disgrace us and say that the Temple was destroyed very quickly, before forty years had passed,[9] because of the guilt of what we had done to him. But this is not so. For his birth was eighty-nine years before the time of birth that they say. The truth is that he was born in the year [three thousand] six hundred and seventy-eight, and he was captured in the year two hundred and ninety-nine from the rebuilding of the Temple, when he was thirty-six years old. This was the third

---

1   *the Nazarene*   Jesus.

2   *Yannai II, who is Alexander*   Alexander Janneaus, King of Judea 103–76 BCE, though Abraham's dates differ.

3   *rebuilding of the Temple*   I.e, the building of the Second Temple. The First Temple was destroyed in 586 BCE, and the rebuilding is now usually set at 516 BCE. Abraham, however, dates it to 352–51 BCE.

4   *fifty-first year of the Hasmoneans*   The Hasmonean dynasty was established in Judea c. 140 BCE.

5   *three thousand six hundred and seventy-eight*   83–82 BCE. Abraham uses the Jewish calendar. 3678 is probably an error for 3672 (90–89 BCE), since Abraham's dating of Jesus' birth and death otherwise consistently amount to an 89-year difference between Jewish and Christian dates.

6   *Herod, ... the Hasmoneans*   Herod the Great. Cf. Matthew 2.

7   *[three thousand] seven hundred and sixty*   1 BCE–1 CE.

8   *the destruction*   I.e., the destruction of the Second Temple in 70 CE. Abraham's date differs slightly.

9   *before forty years had passed*   Cf. *Siege* lines 21–24.

year of Aristobulus, the son of Yannai.[1] Because of this, the sages of Israel have written in a disputation they had with the Christians that the Nazarene that they talk about is not mentioned in the Talmud.[2] Also in the histories of the Christians there is a disagreement about the year in which he was born.

1   *Aristobulus, the son of Yannai*   Aristobulus II, High Priest and King of Judea 66–63 BCE. Abraham's dates differ.

2   *Because of this ... Talmud*   I.e., Because of the dating discrepancies, rabbis can argue that the Jesus mentioned in the Talmud is not the same Jesus that Christians talk about. This argument was indeed used to answer Christian charges against the Talmud. See John Friedman's translation of "The Disputation of Rabbi Yehiel of Paris" in *The Trial of the Talmud: Paris, 1240* (Toronto: Pontifical Institute for Medieval Studies, 2012), 138–39.

Works Cited and Recommended Reading

Editions of *The Siege of Jerusalem*

Hanna, Ralph, and David Lawton, eds. *The Siege of Jerusalem*. EETS OS 320. Oxford: Oxford UP, 2003.

Kölbing, Eugen, and Mabel Day, eds. *The Siege of Jerusalem*. EETS OS 188. London: Oxford UP, 1932.

Livingston, Michael, ed. *Siege of Jerusalem*. TEAMS Middle English Texts Series. Kalamazoo, MI: Medieval Institute, 2004.

Turville-Petre, Thorlac, ed. "The Siege of Jerusalem (ll. 521–724)." *Alliterative Poetry of the Later Middle Ages: An Anthology*. Ed. Thorlac Turville-Petre. London: Routledge, 1989. 158–69.

Other Primary Sources

Amichai, Yehuda. *Open Closed Open*. Trans. Chana Bloch and Chana Kronfeld. New York: Harcourt, 2000.

Andrew, Malcolm, and Ronald Waldron, eds. *The Poems of the Pearl Manuscript: Pearl, Cleanness, Patience, Sir Gawain and the Green Knight*. 5th ed. Exeter Medieval Texts and Studies. Exeter: U of Exeter P, 2008.

Cornfeld, Gaalya, ed. and trans. *Josephus: The Jewish War*. Grand Rapids, MI: Zondervan, 1982.

D'Evelyn, Charlotte, and Anna J. Mill, eds. *The South English Legendary*. 2 vols. EETS OS 235–6. London: Oxford UP, 1956.

Douay-Rheims Holy Bible. Fitzwilliam, NH: Loreto, 2000.

Duggan, Hoyt N., and Thorlac Turville-Petre, eds. *The Wars of Alexander*. EETS SS 10. Oxford: Oxford UP, 1989.

Ehrman, Bart D., and Zlatko Plese, ed. and trans. *The Apocryphal Gospels: Texts and Translations*. Oxford and New York: Oxford UP, 2011.

Eidelberg, Shlomo, ed. and trans. *The Jews and the Crusaders: The Hebrew Chronicles of the First and Second Crusades*. Hoboken, NJ: KTAV, 1996.

Erbe, Theodor, ed. *Mirk's Festial: A Collection of Homilies by Johannes Mirkus.* EETS ES 96. London: Kegan Paul, 1905.

Ford, Alvin E., ed. *La Vengeance de Nostre-Seigneur: The Old and Middle French Prose Versions.* Studies and Texts 63, 115. Toronto: Pontifical Institute, 1984–93.

Friedman, John, and Jean Connell Hoff, trans. *The Trial of the Talmud: Paris, 1240.* Intro. by Robert Chazan. Medieval Sources in Translation. Toronto: Pontifical Institute for Medieval Studies, 2012.

Galloway, Andrew, ed. "Appendix: John of Tynemouth's Account of the Siege of Jerusalem," in "Alliterative Poetry in Old Jerusalem: *The Siege of Jerusalem* and Its Sources." *Medieval Alliterative Poetry: Essays in Honour of Thorlac Turville-Petre.* Ed. John A. Burrow and Hoyt N. Duggan. Dublin: Four Courts, 2010. 96–106.

Habermann, A.M., ed. *Sefer Gezerot Ashkenaz ve-Zorfat* [*Book of Persecutions in Germany and France*]. Jerusalem: Tarshish, 1945.

Hamel, Mary, ed. *Morte Arthure: A Critical Edition.* Garland Medieval Texts 9. New York and London: Garland, 1984.

Herbert, J.A., ed. *Titus & Vespasian: or, The Destruction of Jerusalem in Rhymed Couplets.* Roxburghe Club 146. London: Roxburghe Club, 1905.

Horstmann, Carl, ed. *The Minor Poems of the Vernon Manuscript.* EETS OS 98. London: Kegan Paul, 1892.

Hulme, William H., ed. *The Middle English Harrowing of Hell and Gospel of Nicodemus.* EETS ES 100. London: Oxford UP, 1907.

Jacobus de Voragine. *The Golden Legend.* Trans. William Granger Ryan. 2 vols. Princeton: Princeton UP, 1993.

Jessop, A., and M.R. James, ed. and trans. *The Life and Miracles of St. William of Norwich.* Cambridge: Cambridge UP, 1896.

Kane, George, and E. Talbot Donaldson, eds. *Piers Plowman: The B Version.* London: Athlone, 1975.

Krey, August Charles, ed. and trans. *The First Crusade: The Accounts of Eyewitnesses and Participants.* Princeton: Princeton UP, 1921.

Kurvinen, Auvo, ed. *The Siege of Jerusalem in Prose.* Mémoires de la Société Néophilologique de Helsinki 34. Helsinki: Société Néophilologique, 1969.

Mandeville, John. *The Book of Marvels and Travels.* Ed. and trans. Anthony Bale. Oxford World's Classics. Oxford: Oxford UP, 2012.

Marcus, Jacob Rader, ed. and trans. *The Jew in the Medieval World: A Source Book: 315–1791*. Rev. ed. by Marc Saperstein. Cincinnati, OH: Hebrew Union College Press, 1999.

Moe, Phyllis, ed. *The Middle English Prose Translations of Roger d'Argenteuil's Bible en françois*. Middle English Texts 6. Heidelberg: Winter, 1977.

Panton, George A., and David Donaldson, eds. *The Gest Hystoriale of the Destruction of Troy*. 2 vols. EETS OS 39, 56. London: Trübner, 1869–74.

Pearsall, David, ed. *Piers Plowman by William Langland: An Edition of the C-Text*. York Medieval Texts, Second Series. Berkeley and Los Angeles: U of California P, 1978.

Sisam, Kenneth, ed. *Fourteenth-Century Verse and Prose*. Oxford: Clarendon, 1921.

"Statute of the Jewry." *Statutes of the Realm, Printed by Command of His Majesty King George the Third in Pursuance of an Address of the House of Commons of Great Britain from Original Records and Authoritative Manuscripts*. Vol. 1. London: 1810. 221–221a.

Turville-Petre, Thorlac, ed. *Alliterative Poetry of the Later Middle Ages: An Anthology*. London: Routledge, 1989.

Whiston, William, trans. *The Complete Works of Flavius Josephus*. London: Nelson, 1860.

Zacuto, Abraham ben Samuel. *Sefer Yuhasin ha-Shalem* [*The Complete Book of Lineage*]. Jerusalem: Yerid ha-Sefarim, 2004.

Scholarship on *The Siege of Jerusalem*

Chism, Christine. "*The Siege of Jerusalem*: Liquidating Assets." *Journal of Medieval and Early Modern Studies* 28.2 (1998): 309–40.

——. "Profiting from Precursors in *The Siege of Jerusalem*." *Alliterative Revivals*. Philadelphia: U of Pennsylvania P, 2002. 155–88.

Diamond, Arlyn. "The Alliterative *Siege of Jerusalem*: The Poetics of Destruction." *Boundaries in Medieval Romance*. Ed. Neil Cartlidge. Studies in Medieval Romance. Cambridge: D.S. Brewer, 2008. 103–14.

Finlayson, John. "The Contexts of the Crusading Romances in the London Thornton Manuscript." *Anglia* 130.2 (2012): 240–63.

Galloway, Andrew. "Alliterative Poetry in Old Jerusalem: *The Siege of Jerusalem* and Its Sources." *Medieval Alliterative Poetry: Essays in Honour of Thorlac Turville-Petre*. Eds. John A. Burrow and Hoyt N. Duggan. Dublin: Four Courts, 2010. 85–106.

Hamel, Mary. "*The Siege of Jerusalem* as a Crusading Poem." *Journeys Toward God: Pilgrimage and Crusade*. Ed. Barbara N. Sargent-Baur. Studies in Medieval Culture 30. Kalamazoo, MI: Medieval Institute, 1992. 177–94.

Hanna, Ralph, III. "Contextualising *The Siege of Jerusalem*." *Yearbook of Langland Studies* 6 (1992): 109–21.

Johnston, Michael. "Robert Thornton and *The Siege of Jerusalem*." *Yearbook of Langland Studies* 23 (2009): 125–62.

Lawton, David. "Titus Goes Hunting and Hawking: The Poetics of Recreation and Revenge in *The Siege of Jerusalem*." *Individuality and Achievement in Middle English Poetry*. Ed. O.S. Pickering. Cambridge: D.S. Brewer, 1997. 105–17.

Millar, Bonnie. "The Role of Prophecy in the *Siege of Jerusalem* and Its Analogues." *Yearbook of Langland Studies* 13 (1999): 153–78.

———. *The Siege of Jerusalem in Its Physical, Literary and Historical Contexts*. Dublin: Four Courts, 2000.

Moe, Phyllis. "The French Source of the Alliterative 'Siege of Jerusalem.'" *Medium Ævum* 39 (1970): 147–54.

Mueller, Alex. "Corporal Terror: Critiques of Imperialism in *The Siege of Jerusalem*." *Philological Quarterly* 84.3 (2005): 287–310.

Nicholson, Roger. "Haunted Itineraries: Reading *The Siege of Jerusalem*." *Exemplaria* 14.2 (2002): 447–84.

Price, Merrall Llewelyn. "Imperial Violence and the Monstrous Mother: Cannibalism at the Siege of Jerusalem." *Domestic Violence in Medieval Texts*. Eds. Eve Salisbury, Georgiana Donavin, and Merrall Llewelyn Price. Gainesville: UP of Florida, 2002. 272–98.

Price, Patricia. "Integrating Time and Space: The Literary Geography of *Patience, Cleanness, The Siege of Jerusalem*, and *St. Erkenwald*." *Medieval Perspectives* 11 (1996): 234–50.

Schiff, Randy P. "The Instructive Other Within: Secularized Jews in *The Siege of Jerusalem*." *Cultural Diversity in the British Middle Ages: Archipelago, Island, England*. Ed. Jeffrey Jerome Cohen. New Middle Ages. New York: Palgrave, 2008. 135–52.

Stinson, Timothy L. "Makeres of the Mind: Authorial Intention, Editorial Practice, and *The Siege of Jerusalem.*" *Yearbook of Langland Studies* 24.1 (2010): 39–62.

Van Court, Elisa Narin. "*The Siege of Jerusalem* and Augustinian Historians: Writing about Jews in Fourteenth-Century England." *Chaucer Review* 29 (1995): 227–48.

———. "*The Siege of Jerusalem* and Recuperative Readings." *Pulp Fictions of Medieval England: Essays in Popular Romance.* Ed. Nicola McDonald. Manchester: Manchester UP, 2004. 151–70.

Yeager, Suzanne M. "*The Siege of Jerusalem* and Biblical Exegesis: Writing about Romans in Fourteenth-Century England." *Chaucer Review* 39.1 (2004): 70–102.

———. "The Crusade of the Soul in *The Siege of Jerusalem.*" *Jerusalem in Medieval Narrative.* Cambridge Studies in Medieval Literature 72. Cambridge: Cambridge UP, 2008. 78–107.

———. "Jewish Identity in *The Siege of Jerusalem* and Homiletic Texts: Models of Penance and Victims of Vengeance for the Urban Apocalypse." *Medieval Ævum* 80.1 (2011): 56–84.

Literary and Historical Contexts

Akbari, Suzanne Conklin. "Placing the Jews in Late Medieval English Literature." *Orientalism and the Jews.* Eds. Ivan Davidson Kalmar and Derek Jonathan Penslar. Tauber Institute Series for the Study of European Jewry. Lebanon, NH: Brandeis UP, 2005. 30–50.

———. "Erasing the Body: History and Memory in Medieval Siege Poetry." *Remembering the Crusades: Myth, Image, and Identity.* Eds. Nicholas Paul and Suzanne Yeager. Baltimore: Johns Hopkins UP, 2012. 146–73.

Bale, Anthony. *The Jew in the Medieval Book: English Antisemitisms, 1350–1500.* Cambridge Studies in Medieval Literature. Cambridge: Cambridge UP, 2006.

———. *Feeling Persecuted: Christians, Jews, and Images of Violence in the Middle Ages.* London: Reaktion, 2010.

Birenbaum, Maija. "Affective Vengeance in *Titus and Vespasian.*" *Chaucer Review* 43.3 (2009): 330–44.

Blurton, Heather. *Cannibalism in High Medieval English Literature.* The New Middle Ages. New York: Palgrave, 2007.

Cable, Thomas. *The English Alliterative Tradition*. Philadelphia: U of Pennsylvania P, 1991.

Chazan, Robert. "Crusading in Christian-Jewish Polemics." *The Medieval Crusade*. Ed. Susan J. Ridyard. Woodbridge: Boydell, 2004. 33–51.

Chism, Christine. *Alliterative Revivals*. Philadelphia: U of Pennsylvania P, 2002.

Cohen, Jeffrey Jerome, ed. *The Postcolonial Middle Ages*. New York: St. Martin's, 2000.

Cohen, Jeremy. *Living Letters of the Law: Ideas of the Jew in Medieval Christianity*. Berkeley: U of California P, 1999.

Delany, Sheila, ed. *Chaucer and the Jews: Sources, Contexts, Meanings*. New York: Routledge, 2002.

Field, Rosalind, Phillipa Hardman, and Michelle Sweeney, eds. *Christianity and Romance in Medieval England*. Cambridge: D.S. Brewer, 2010.

Gransden, Antonia. *Historical Writing in England*. 2 vols. London: Routledge and Kegan Paul, 1974–82.

Hanna, Ralph, III. "Alliterative Poetry." *The Cambridge History of Medieval English Literature*. Cambridge: Cambridge UP, 1999. 488–512.

Hebron, Malcolm. *The Medieval Siege: Theme and Image in Middle English Romance*. Oxford: Clarendon, 1997.

Heng, Geraldine. "The Romance of England: Richard Coer de Lyon, Saracens, Jews, and the Politics of Race and Nation." *The Postcolonial Middle Ages*. Ed. Jeffrey Jerome Cohen. New York: St Martin's, 2000. 135–71.

Hyams, Paul, and Susanna A. Throop. *Vengeance in the Middle Ages: Emotion, Religion, and Feud*. Farnham, UK: Ashgate, 2010.

Jacobs, Nicholas. "Alliterative Storms: A Topos in Middle English." *Speculum* 47 (1972): 695–719.

Keen, Maurice H. *The Laws of War in the Late Middle Ages*. London: Routledge and Kegan Paul, 1965.

Kruger, Steven F. "Bodies of Jews in the Middle Ages." *The Idea of Medieval Literature: Essays on Chaucer and Medieval Culture in Honor of Donald R. Howard*. Eds. James M. Dean and Christian K. Zacher. Newark: U of Delaware P, 1992. 307–23.

——. *The Spectral Jew: Conversion and Embodiment in Medieval Europe*. Minneapolis, MN: U of Minnesota P, 2006.

Krummel, Miriamne Ara. *Crafting Jewishness in Medieval England: Legally Absent, Virtually Present.* The New Middle Ages. New York: Palgrave, 2010.

Lampert[-Weissig], Lisa R. *Gender and Jewish Difference from Paul to Shakespeare.* Middle Ages Series. Philadelphia: U of Pennsylvania P, 2004.

Langmuir, Gavin. *Toward a Definition of Antisemitism.* Berkeley and Los Angeles: U of California P, 1990.

Lawton, David, ed. *Middle English Alliterative Poetry and Its Literary Background.* Cambridge: D.S. Brewer, 1982.

Levine, Lee I. *Jerusalem: Its Sanctity and Centrality to Judaism, Christianity, and Islam.* New York: Continuum, 1999.

Linder, Amnon. "Jews and Judaism in the Eyes of Christian Thinkers of the Middle Ages: The Destruction of Jerusalem in Medieval Christian Liturgy." *From Witness to Witchcraft: Jews and Judaism in Medieval Christian Thought.* Ed. Jeremy Cohen. Wolfenbütteler Mittelalter-Studien 11. Wiesbaden: Harrassowitz, 1996. 113–23.

McDonald, Nicola, ed. *Pulp Fictions of Medieval England: Essays in Popular Romance.* Manchester: Manchester UP, 2004.

Mehl, Dieter. *The Middle English Romances of the Thirteenth and Fourteenth Centuries.* London: Routledge and Kegan Paul, 1968.

Morey, James. *Book and Verse: A Guide to Middle English Biblical Literature.* Urbana: U of Illinois P, 2000.

Mundill, Robin R. *England's Jewish Solution: Experiment and Expulsion, 1262–1290.* Cambridge Studies in Medieval Life and Thought. Cambridge: Cambridge UP, 1998.

——. *The King's Jews: Money, Massacre, and Exodus in Medieval England.* London and New York: Continuum, 2010.

Nirenberg, David. *Anti-Judaism: The Western Tradition.* New York and London: Norton, 2013.

Putter, Ad, Judith Jefferson, and Myra Stokes. *Studies in the Metre of Alliterative Verse.* Medium Ævum Monographs n.s. 25. Oxford: Society for the Study of Medieval Languages and Literature, 2007.

Riley-Smith, Jonathan. "Christian Violence and the Crusades." *Religious Violence between Christians and Jews: Medieval Roots, Modern*

Perspectives. Ed. Anna Sapir Abulafia. New York: Palgrave, 2002. 3–20.

———. *What Were the Crusades?* 3rd ed. San Francisco: Ignatius, 2002.

Rubin, Miri. *Gentile Tales: The Narrative Assault on Late Medieval Jews.* New Haven, CT: Yale UP, 1999.

Spearing, A.C. "Alliterative Poetry." *Readings in Medieval Poetry.* Cambridge: Cambridge UP, 1987. 134–73.

Stacey, Robert. "From Ritual Murder to Host Desecration: Jews and the Body of Christ." *Jewish History* 12.1 (1998): 11–28.

———. "Crusades, Martyrdoms, and the Jews of Norman England, 1096–1190." *Juden und Christen zur Zeit der Kreuzzüge.* Ed. Alfred Haverkamp. Vorträge und Forschungen 47. Sigmaringen: Thorbecke, 1999. 233–51.

Turville-Petre, Thorlac. *The Alliterative Revival.* Cambridge: D.S. Brewer, 1977.

Tyerman, Christopher. *England and the Crusades, 1098–1588.* Chicago: U of Chicago P, 1988.

Van Court, Elisa Narin. "Socially Marginal, Culturally Central: Representing Jews in Late Medieval English Literature." *Exemplaria* 12.2 (2000): 293–326.

Williams Boyarin, Adrienne. *Miracles of the Virgin in Medieval England: Law and Jewishness in Marian Legends.* Cambridge: D.S. Brewer, 2010.

Wright, Stephen K. *The Vengeance of Our Lord: Medieval Dramatizations of the Destruction of Jerusalem.* Studies and Texts 89. Toronto: Pontifical Institute, 1989.

Yeager, Suzanne M. *Jerusalem in Medieval Narrative.* Cambridge Studies in Medieval Literature 72. Cambridge: Cambridge UP, 2008.

Yuval, Israel Jacob. *Two Nations in Our Womb: Perceptions of Jews and Christians in Late Antiquity and the Middle Ages.* Trans. Barbara Harshaw and Jonathan Chipman. Berkeley: U of California P, 2006.

From the Publisher

A name never says it all, but the word "Broadview" expresses a good deal of the philosophy behind our company. We are open to a broad range of academic approaches and political viewpoints. We pay attention to the broad impact book publishing and book printing has in the wider world; for some years now we have used 100% recycled paper for most titles. Our publishing program is internationally oriented and broad-ranging. Our individual titles often appeal to a broad readership too; many are of interest as much to general readers as to academics and students.

Founded in 1985, Broadview remains a fully independent company owned by its shareholders—not an imprint or subsidiary of a larger multinational.

For the most accurate information on our books (including information on pricing, editions, and formats) please visit our website at www.broadviewpress.com. Our print books and ebooks are also available for sale on our site.

broadview press
www.broadviewpress.com

This book is made of paper from well-managed FSC® - certified
forests, recycled materials, and other controlled sources.